GLEEFUL!

A TOTALLY UNOFFICIAL GUIDE
TO THE HIT TV SERIES GLEE

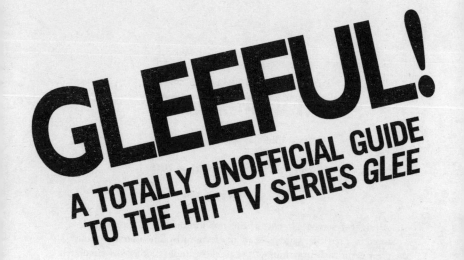

GLEEFUL!

A TOTALLY UNOFFICIAL GUIDE TO THE HIT TV SERIES GLEE

AMY RICKMAN

JB

JOHN BLAKE

Published by John Blake Publishing Ltd,
3 Bramber Court, 2 Bramber Road,
London W14 9PB, England

www.johnblakepublishing.co.uk

First published in paperback in 2010

ISBN: 978 1 84358 169 7

British Library Cataloguing-in-Publication Data:

A catalogue record for this book is available from the British Library.

Design by www.envydesign.co.uk

Printed in Great Britain by CPI Bookmarque, Croydon, CR0 4TD

1 3 5 7 9 10 8 6 4 2

As the title makes clear, this is a totally unofficial guide to the hit
television show, *Glee*. We hope you find it useful and that it encourages
you to continue watching the show.

Papers used by John Blake Publishing are natural, recyclable products
made from wood grown in sustainable forests. The manufacturing processes
conform to the environmental regulations of the country of origin.

For Mum and Dad, who never stop believing

CONTENTS

INTRODUCTION

When a show has the ability to coin a brand new word exclusively to describe its fans, there can be no doubt about its success. And if you happen to be a certified 'Gleek', then *Glee*'s appeal will be of no mystery whatsoever to you! With its strong cast, hilariously witty dialogue, a high-school setting ripe with drama and – of course – a fantastic songbook packed to the brim with Broadway tunes and hits from every genre and decade, *Glee* is a universal crowd-pleaser. But it wasn't always so cut and dry: for every *Glee,* there's a musical show like *Cop Rock* or *Britannia High* that never manages to get off the ground. So what sets *Glee* apart from the rest?

It helps that every *Glee* cast member knew something

special was happening on the set. From the beginning, they realised as they were filming that they were creating something truly magical. There's a real sense of excitement when you hear the actors talk about their work, and it's not just because it's their first job – although for most of them it is their first real television gig. It's because their characters speak to them in a way that hasn't been done before. Ryan Murphy, Ian Brennan and Brad Falchuk have captured the voice of a generation, with all its wit and quirk and self-esteem issues. We've entered an era where it's way more cool to be square, where geek really *is* the new chic, and where a weekend at San Francisco Comic-Con gets more respect than a day out shopping in Beverly Hills.

Finally, TV scriptwriters and producers are realising that teens are *smart* and they want television writing that respects them. The major TV networks are also becoming more aware that there are other ways to interact with this savvy audience than just through the screen. Social networks, Twitter, Tumblr, Facebook, podcasts, YouTube videos, Hulu, Wikipedia, iTunes, flash mobs – they all add up to transform the marketing industry. No wonder *Glee* is doing so well; the marketing teams have been working in overdrive to innovate their advertising campaigns. No one has been content to use the 'regular' methods when it comes to *Glee*. One pilot wasn't enough – there were three. The *Glee*-cast singles, released simultaneously with the airing of the shows, hit the charts internationally. Fans from every corner of the globe uploaded videos of themselves singing their own covers of 'Don't Stop Believin'' and that's when the producers knew they had struck a gold mine with *Glee*.

It seems the musical genre is back and thriving, hitting the big and small screens in a huge way, with *Mamma Mia!*, *Nine* and of course, *High School Musical*, drawing in massive audiences. Musicals demand so much of the actors who star in them. Although Ryan Murphy claims to have been inspired by the reality TV talent show *American Idol*, *Glee* is the very antithesis of the assembly line of singers churned out by the *Idol* and *X-Factor*-style hit-making factories. A large proportion of the *Glee* cast have come straight from Broadway or, if they were newly discovered, have all the talent to perform in front of a live audience.

Gleeful! A Totally Unofficial Guide to the Hit TV series Glee charts the show's history, from a spark in Ian Brennan's mind through to Ryan Murphy's slickly conceived pilot episode. You can also read all about the cast members and how they became part of this musical television phenomenon. And, if you want to relive your favourite *Glee* scenes all over again, check out the episode guides, which feature tidbits of trivia and point out those little '*Gleeful!* Moments' that you might have missed first time around.

The curtain's up…

A HIGH SCHOOL GLOSSARY

Love the show, but maybe you're unfamiliar with some of the American High School terms? Decode some of the lingo here.

High School
Junior High – Years 7 & 8
Freshman – Year 9
Sophomore – Year 10
Junior – Year 11
Senior – Year 12

A WHO'S WHO
OF *GLEE*

William McKinley High Faculty
Principal Figgins – Iqbal Theba
Will Schuester – Matthew Morrison
Emma Pillsbury – Jayma Mays
Ken Tanaka – Patrick Gallagher
Sandy Ryerson – Stephen Tobolowsky
Sue Sylvester – Jane Lynch

New Directions
Rachel Berry – Lea Michele
Finn Hudson – Cory Monteith
Kurt Hummel – Chris Colfer
Artie Abrams – Kevin McHale
Mercedes Jones – Amber Riley
Tina Cohen-Chang – Jenna Ushkowitz

Quinn Fabray – Dianna Agron

Noah 'Puck' Puckerman – Mark Salling

Mike Chang – Harry Shum Jr.

Matt Rutherford – Dijon Talton

Santana Lopez – Naya Rivera

Brittany – Heather Morris

Other Lima, Ohio Residents

Terri Schuester – Jessalyn Gilsig

Jacob Ben Israel – Josh Sussman

CHAPTER 1
GLEE IS OUTED

When the pilot episode for *Glee* aired on 29 May 2009 in the prime ratings spot following *American Idol*, Ryan Murphy, Brad Falchuk and Ian Brennan anxiously awaited the public's reaction. The three creators of the show simply didn't know what to expect. So would America take to their darkly comedic vision of an all-singing, all-dancing band of social misfits? Would they see it for the hilarious, original show it was, or take it for a *High School Musical* rip-off? And most importantly of all, would they want to see more?

At first, Murphy wasn't sure about the post-*Idol* time slot. He could see the merit in putting the two music shows together as much of the audience was bound to crossover. But *Glee* wasn't officially planned to première until

September 2009 – three months after *American Idol*. He spoke with Terry Gross on National Public Radio about hearing the news for the first time from the executives at FOX. 'And I said: "Well, I don't know." That seems a little scary to me because, you know, then the show will be off the air for three months. It doesn't make sense to me.'

Luckily, Murphy got over his reservations and the planned pilot went ahead. It had to be edited down to fit the 47-minute window after *Idol*, but as far as the taster that the audience had? They loved it. Unequivocally. *Glee* was an instant hit, and audiences hadn't even seen a full episode yet.

But Murphy and Falchuk were no strangers to television success. Murphy was already an experienced television producer. Born in 1966 in Indianapolis, Indiana, he was the precocious child of a housewife mother and semi-pro hockey player dad. He came out to his parents when he was 15 years old, but his dad had already been bemused by some of his son's earliest quirks – like asking for a subscription to *Vogue* magazine when he was 5 years old, not to mention his growing love of musical theatre. 'My dad would look at me and go, "What the hell? I don't know who you are! How did you come out of me?" He would say things like that,' Murphy recalled. But he was fully accepted by his parents and never experienced any of the taunting that many gay kids have to endure in high school. Instead he

2

was popular and well liked. He sang in his church choir – an experience that would inform him down the line with *Glee* – and performed in as many of his school's musical theatre performances as possible.

After graduating from college, Murphy started his first job as a journalist, working as the entertainment reporter in Hollywood for the *Miami Herald*. He ended up staying out in Los Angeles and worked for the *Los Angeles Times* and *Entertainment Weekly*. Eventually he realised that he wanted to be on the other side of the business – actually scripting the shows, not just writing about them. His first script, *Why Can't I Be Audrey Hepburn?*, was bought by Steven Spielberg, although it was never made. It was a remarkable launch into the biz.

By 1999, Murphy broke into television with the teen comedy series, *Popular*. The show is about two girls on opposite ends of the popularity spectrum forced to live together when their single parents meet each other and marry. *Popular* became something of a cult hit, although it never fully took off with mainstream audiences.

In fact, it was Murphy's former career as a journalist that helped create his biggest hit show pre-*Glee*. He was asked to go undercover and write an article about plastic surgery in Beverly Hills. Although he was fully prepared to write a sarcastic piece on how people get sucked into making drastic changes to their bodies, when he actually met the doctor, he himself started to fall for the sales pitch.

The result of the meeting was not an article – in fact, Murphy never wrote it – but the kernel of an idea. And what came out of that idea was *Nip/Tuck*, an hour-long TV drama that revealed the sinister side of plastic surgery. The show's signature line – 'Tell me what you don't like about yourself' – was precisely what the doctor that Murphy visited had said to him, and the line quickly embedded itself in American popular culture. *Nip/Tuck* enjoyed a run of seven seasons, ending on 3 March 2010, and it became well known for its graphic depictions of plastic surgeries.

Murphy insisted on the violence of the surgeries being as realistic as possible but to warn squeamish viewers, he played a specific musical track so that people would know when the gory stuff was on its way: '[The surgeries are] horrific, and violent, and scary, and to the point that you know we devise the show for the audience,' he said, live on air on National Public Radio. 'You know a surgery is coming when you have a Bang & Olufsen CD player, when they open up that CD player to put that CD in because we always score those surgeries to pop music. A lot of people say to me "I know that's where I have to either fast forward through or I'll turn away, or I'll go into the kitchen and get something to eat because the surgeries are pretty in your face."'

Brad Falchuk interviewed with Ryan Murphy for a role on *Nip/Tuck* and came aboard as one of the writers.

Together they formed a close partnership, which also saw them write a pilot for a TV series about transsexuals called *Pretty/Handsome* although this was never picked up by a network. With *Nip/Tuck* winding down, they started the hunt for their next script, something a bit more light-hearted this time around. 'We jokingly say [*Nip/Tuck*] is set over the big mouth of the gates of hell,' said Murphy. 'It's so dark. And I wanted to do something more hopeful because everybody thinks I'm such a dark person and I really feel that I'm not... I think that now people maybe want something that makes [people] smile and feel good.' What's more, he was looking for a project where he could share his love of music. He was already embarking on an ambitious filmmaking project, bringing the bestselling book *Eat, Pray, Love* by Elizabeth Gilbert to life on the big screen with Julia Roberts. 'Everybody thinks I'm the dark prince of television,' he commented to *Billboard.com*. 'But I was at a point where I wanted to do something light. I've always been very into music, and I wanted to show that.'

In fact, their timing couldn't have been better for actor and first-time screenwriter Ian Brennan, who was based out of Chicago and New York. He studied theatre at Loyola University Chicago and worked with the Goodman and Steppenwolf theatre companies in Chicago (another Steppenwolf alum is *Glee* star Jane

Lynch). Brennan had enjoyed small success in the acting world and appeared in the off-Broadway play *The Man in the White Suit* (2006).

But something kept drawing him back to his memories of high school or, more specifically, his high-school Glee Club. Brennan attended Prospect High School in Mt Prospect, just outside Chicago, in the 1990s and was an active member of the show choir. In fact, he loathed the experience and only joined because he wanted to be an actor – and the same teacher who oversaw show choir cast all the parts in their amateur theatre. '[O]ur show choir performances were things that I just wanted to survive. I have one hilarious videotape where I'm in a terrible tuxedo, and my hair is awful, and I'm zitty and way too thin,' he told *Chicago Tribune*.

Nevertheless, something about the emotional highs and lows, the highly choreographed dance moves and the overly-sequined outfits struck a chord with Brennan and he realised there was a great story to be uncovered, one that had never been told before. Sure, movies such as *Bring It On* (2000) had glamorised competitive cheerleading while *Drumline* (2002) showcased marching bands, but there was nothing of the kind about show choir. The kids who joined show choir were unique: they were all searching for something, a place to express themselves through song and dance on a glitzy stage a world away from their perhaps humdrum lives.

'I find it interesting that there is something in everybody, a longing for something transcendent, particularly in a place like Mt. Prospect, a place that's very suburban and normal and plain. Even in places like that, there's this desire to shine. That's fascinating and very funny to me, especially when people try to accomplish this through show choir – which, to me, is inherently a little ridiculous,' he observed.

It was an opportunity Brennan knew he had to seize before someone else got there first – 'I figured if I didn't write it, someone else would, and then I'd always be kicking myself.'

So, in August 2005, he went out to the bookstore, purchased *Screenwriting for Dummies*, and got straight to work. 'I had never written much besides some sketch stuff in high school and some terrible plays in college,' he later admitted. Obviously that didn't hold him back, and he penned what would turn out to be the very first incarnation of *Glee*... a movie.

With the benefit of hindsight and knowing how successful *Glee* has become, you might be forgiven for thinking that Brennan would have had no trouble selling his script, which 'featured teacher-student sex and a character addicted to Demerol'. The reality was that he shopped the concept for nearly two years without a single bite of interest. Eventually, he partnered up with a friend, Mike Novack, who happened to belong to the same gym as Ryan Murphy. Novack offered the script to Murphy saying, 'I don't know you, but I know your work, but I'm taking a guess that you were in Glee Club... My partner Ian [Brennan] and I have an idea for a movie that we would want you to produce.'

As it turned out, Novack had finally placed the script in the right hands. 'I get this world,' said Murphy once he had read through the script. Not only did he understand Glee Clubs and the world Brennan was writing about, but he had a vision for the best possible medium in which to produce the work: television. It was exactly what he and Brad Falchuk had been looking for, and Murphy loved the title, which he saw as referring to 'malicious optimism' – a phrase that would come to define the tone of the show. So they went back to Ian Brennan with the idea for a series. Brennan, needless to say, was thrilled to have found two people who were willing to work with him on the script. 'I was excited about that idea, so we basically went about rewriting the whole thing from scratch,' he recalled.

The concept they came up with was simple, but brilliant. The show would be a one-hour comedy set in a high school, featuring five to seven songs per episode. There would be no original music (at least not initially) and instead they would pull from all genres of popular songs, which they would rearrange to fit their ensemble cast and then professionally record in a studio. And just like that, they opened up an entirely new revenue stream for a network: single-track iTunes downloads of the music featured on the show, instantly available the moment each episode ended.

Murphy and Brennan pitched the idea to executives at the American television network FOX and they loved it. Everything had come together at the right time. Already FOX had experienced a lot of success with *American Idol* and had seen how, in Britain, the winner of *X Factor* benefited from having a single ready for instant download. From 2005–08, every winner of the *X Factor* achieved the No. 1 single at Christmas. The same couldn't be said for *American Idol*, however, and FOX knew they had an unexplored avenue available to them. The trouble was, they needed the right show. And then along came *Glee*...

Of course, it was still a big gamble. Musical television shows have a chequered history. Some were hugely popular, like *Fame* in the 1980s. Others have fallen flat on their faces. *Cop Rock* was an American TV series in the 1990s that presented a police drama as a musical and was recently voted 8th Worst TV Show of all Time by *TV Guide*. And *Viva Laughlin* (2007), which starred Hugh Jackman, was cancelled after only two episodes. In Britain, music TV has fared marginally better. In fact, both *Cop Rock* and *Viva Laughlin* were inspired by BBC original shows, *The Singing Detective* (2003) and *Viva*

Blackpool (2006) respectively. Still, it had been a long time since any scripted series featuring music had been a success. It was a challenging formula: not only did the songs have to appeal to the nation but the dialogue, plot and the characters must also be spot-on.

Even that might not have been enough without the right kind of support from the television network. There are plenty of examples of shows with great writing, witty dialogue and big-name stars that just haven't been able to connect with audiences and so they flounder. *Pushing Daisies*, *Arrested Development* and *Dollhouse* all had great critical reviews but none of the ratings. There is obviously a myriad of factors that contribute to this, but in the US, poor ratings often have a lot to do with timing. Often a Friday-night spot would sound the death knell for a series, whereas Thursdays were a ratings boon.

Luckily for *Glee*, the network execs *got it*. Murphy is especially grateful for their support. 'I thought *Glee* was good, and I thought *Glee* was original,' he said, 'but when you do those things on TV, half the time it doesn't work so I was always startled by how much FOX got behind it. They really put the muscle to it and launched it correctly and creatively, so people found it and loved it.'

But they were also willing to put their money where their mouths were. Each episode costs as estimated $3 million to produce, around 50 per cent more than a regular primetime show. This accounts for the additional cost of the elaborate choreography, recording studio time and clearing music rights that most other shows don't need. Additionally, each episode takes ten days to shoot – that's 25 per cent longer than the average show – to give the cast enough time to learn all the dances and rehearse.

So they had the network's approval, the marketing plan and – most importantly – the budget. Now it was up to Murphy, Brennan and Falchuk to make the vision a reality.

Brennan was the most experienced of the three when it came to the ins and outs of Glee Clubs, although Murphy had some experience as well. The team then took to YouTube and watched videos of some of the top-ranked show choirs in the Midwest, and what they saw astounded them. They brought in one of the teams to work on the pilot. 'I mean, we were working with a choir... from Burbank, who I think literally would spend $100,000 a year on costumes and sets in production value,' said Murphy. '[T]hey had... one woman who was a full-time sequin-sewer.' The team became the inspiration for Vocal Adrenaline, the showy rivals of William McKinley High's New Directions club. They set the show in Lima, Ohio in the Midwest as Murphy grew up in Indiana – another Midwestern state – and has lots of good memories of travelling to Ohio to visit the Kings Island theme park.

11

Penning the script was a lot of fun, too. For Falchuk, who was used to writing for *Nip/Tuck*, *Glee* was like a breath of fresh air. With *Nip/Tuck*, 'the idea was always, "What's the cynical turn to the story? What's the dark turn?" With *Glee*, it was the opposite... really embrace how great it is to sing and dance and how great it feels to express yourself.'

And they were keen to make sure the show wasn't about being the biggest and the best. The Vocal Adrenaline-style choreography was great, but there's no fun in writing a storyline solely about a team who wins all the time. Instead, they were keen to tell the tale of 'the world's worst Glee Club' – about the underdogs of the high-school social scene. This would be a show for the losers, the freaks and the geeks of the world.

Little did they realise that they would soon be writing for a previously unnamed group – one hungry for a smart, funny television show that they could sing along to and embrace with a fervour never before known in the TV world: the Gleeks.

CHAPTER TWO

A BRIEF HISTORY OF GLEE CLUBS

*G*lee mania might be gripping the world, but many Gleeks outside the American Midwest have never heard of a 'Glee Club'. However, Glee Clubs are historically a very English tradition and despite the happy, smiling faces of the cast, the term 'glee' has nothing to do with mood of the singers or of the music.

The first recorded Glee Club was founded as far back as 1787, with the creation of the London Glee Club. This was a group of predominantly male singers who got together to sing a 'glee' – a short piece of music written for three or four solo voices to sing without accompaniment. The first song to be defined as a 'glee' was 'Turn, Amaryllis, to thy Swain' by Thomas Brewer. Glees typically expressed idyllic sentiments or were odes to friendship and brotherhood. As they could be sung by more than one person, this type of musical composition gave greater room for expression and creativity than had ever existed before.

The new form of musical group proved extremely popular in the UK in the early 1800s and many clubs formed throughout the country. By 1850, however, choral music began to take over and most of the Glee Clubs closed to make room for choruses. By the early twentieth century, hardly any of the original clubs were left in Great Britain.

Glee Clubs weren't about to give up so easily, though and found life on the other side of the Atlantic. At the height of their English popularity the trend was picked up by Americans and the Harvard Glee Club was founded in 1858. The Harvard club remains in existence today and is still made up of all-male singers: '60 Men – One Voice' proclaims the Harvard Glee Club website, and it has a long and illustrious history. As well as many alumni who went on to become highly influential on the American music scene, it can count two US Presidents – Theodore Roosevelt and Franklin D. Roosevelt – among former members.

With its six-figure yearly budget and preference for Renaissance and folk music, the Harvard Glee Club and its other university counterparts bear little resemblance to the Kanye West-rapping, Broadway musical-singing high-school Glee Club we tune in to watch, week after week. It wasn't until the 1960s, when two separate groups of singers and dancers, 'Up with People' and 'The Young

Americans', began to tour the US that Glee Clubs as we've come to know and love them really began to flourish. More commonly known as 'show choirs', as they combine choral singing with dance, students and teachers would see these two groups perform and be inspired to start a club within their own high school.

GLEEFUL! MOMENT

The pianist accompanying 'New Directions' on the show is *Glee*'s actual music coach Brad Ellis.

The first show choir competition (more commonly known as an 'invitationals', although the competitions are rarely invite-only) was held in 1974 at Bishop Luers High School in Fort Wayne, Indiana and a rulebook for show choirs had to be written. Although rules still differ from state to state (there's no standard rulebook like the one picked up from the library by Sue Sylvester in the pilot episode), most show choirs consist of between 30 and 60 students – far more than the 12 who form 'New Directions'. In addition to the singers and dancers, choirs need to have their own back-up band and behind-the-scenes technical team composed entirely of high-school students, with only a few adult supervisors allowed.

Show choirs gained massive popularity in the US

through the seventies and eighties, particularly in California and the Midwestern states (Illinois, Indiana, Iowa, Kansas, Michigan, Minnesota, Missouri, Nebraska, North Dakota, South Dakota, Ohio and Wisconsin). Standards of competition rose as more schools followed the trend, while budgets swelled to accommodate the need for better costumes, more elaborate props, extensive travel costs and expensive licensing fees for the music. Nowadays, the arrangement and customisation of a particular number for a show choir can cost upwards of $400 – and that's before the fees of any vocal coaches or choreographers. Top show choir students are trained in dance and use classical, swing and tap dancing in their routines, on top of hip-hop and more modern dance.

Some of the biggest competitions – the infamous 'Nationals' – draw over 7,000 spectators and can last several days. These events are extremely prestigious and take place in large venues using professional lighting and sound. Unlike *Glee*, there isn't one single 'National' competition but rather several claiming to find the best show choir in America. In any case, winning one of the big competitions is enough to bring much pride and honour to the Championship school.

So, is Glee Club or show choir really the last resort for nerds and losers at the bottom of the high-school caste system, as depicted on the show? One high-school senior told the *Lee Newspapers* in Wisconsin: 'We don't get slushied or made fun of that much. And there are a lot more people in it, so there's a lot of people to back you up, if something should start.' Safety in numbers is obviously the motto for Glee Club participants yet many famous actors and musicians performed in their high-school show choir, including *Glee*'s Jenna Ushkowitz, *Punk'd* creator Ashton Kutcher, Lance Bass of 'NSync and Blake Lively of *Gossip Girl*.

With such illustrious alumni, it's obvious that being in show choir doesn't necessarily make anyone a loser.

How else does New Directions differ from real life? For one thing, *Glee*'s kids are often handed a brand new piece of sheet music only to perfect their routine in the same rehearsal. 'It takes months of rehearsals to polish a routine and get it up to performance standard,' another senior told *Lee Newspapers*. 'Some of my students get frustrated because [*Glee*] doesn't show all the hard work needed to be successful in show choir,' said high-school choral director Sarah Michael to Chicago's *Daily Herald*.

But, in general, the feeling from both students and administrators in high schools across the US is *Glee* has been a great thing for show choirs. Steve Sivak, choral director at Palatine High School in Chicago, Illinois, followed Sarah Michael's comments by saying that his students 'like the fact that it's bringing notoriety to choral programs in schools and they like the music a lot.'

Some people even believe that *Glee* doesn't go far enough in describing just how passionate people can be about show choir competitions. 'The people who take show choir really, really seriously – they can be really more extreme than depicted on the show,' said Tom King Clear, musical director of Noble Fool Theatricals Youth Ensemble's show choir. And it's not just the students. 'Some of those national competitions are just crazy because the directors are so competitive,' he continued, though he insists those experiences hadn't resulted from his current job but from what he had witnessed while working with show choirs in Missouri and Oregon.

Since the première of *Glee*, show choirs are enjoying something of a renaissance. 'I can't even tell you the number of times kids have come up to me to say that they've started a Glee Club at their school,' said Amber Riley (Mercedes). The clubs are able to provide a valuable creative outlet for kids who might not otherwise get a chance to explore their musical talents.

One establishment in particular – Prospect High School just outside of Chicago, the alma mater of *Glee* creator Ian Brennan – is particularly proud of the show's success. All of a sudden, kids are realising that show choir is actually pretty cool and they want to join in. 'And we're like, "Yeah, we know!"' said Prospect's choral director Jennifer L. Troiano. 'We've been saying that for the past ten years!'

CHAPTER THREE

TEASING AND PLEASING: BUILDING THE BUZZ

There's no doubt about it, *Glee* has captured the world's imagination. Rarely does a show generate such an enormous buzz, not only in the North American states but also in Australia, Great Britain, Europe and Japan. And it has all happened in under a year.

The buzz began with the US TV network FOX's inspired decision to air the pilot of *Glee* after the final performance episode of *American Idol* on 19 May 2009. *American Idol*'s final performance normally draws more than 27 million viewers and even a small share of that kind of audience would be more than the producers could hope for with a new show. In the event, approximately 9.6 million saw the pilot, a very successful turnout for *Glee*. But the strategy wasn't just about getting as many people to watch the show as possible: it was the launch of a huge, elaborate marketing plan – something that had never been attempted for a new television series.

'The way we're looking at May 19 is, it's the world's largest grassroots screening,' Joe Earley, the executive VP in charge of marketing for FOX, told *TV Week*. 'The show sells itself better than any [campaign] can.' Not only that, but after the pilot was aired for the first time, FOX put it on their website, on Hulu (a website that offers streaming of TV shows and movies and allows commercials) and on iTunes so that audiences could watch it free of charge. Word of mouth would sell the product just as much as anything else: they wanted people around the water-cooler to say, 'Hey, have you seen this great new show, *Glee*?' and then for the uninitiated to have a place to go and watch it right away. 'Our goal is to turn the people who watched it into brand ambassadors, to use hackneyed marketing-speak,' continued Joe Earley. 'We believe that when you watch this show, you can't help but get out the word.'

And even the hardest audience to please – the critics – was dying to get the word out. The reviews were packed with effusive praise which transcended even FOX's expectations. Joe Earley is rumoured to have said that he couldn't have written better reviews himself.

The *San Francisco Chronicle* wrote: '*Glee* is infectious and hilarious and oddly inspiring.' *Entertainment*

Weekly was even more fulsome, saying: '[T]his comedy from creator Ryan Murphy (*Nip/Tuck*) is so good – so funny, so bulging with vibrant characters – that it blasts past any defenses you might put up against it. *Glee* will not stop until it wins you over utterly.'

Anyone would be happy with that kind of praise and the buzz for *Glee* got off to a flying start. Ryan Murphy was blown away by the response: 'It's been nothing but positive and fantastic and so gratifying and rewarding for us because we're in this little bubble, shooting all these episodes, and we don't really get to see what people feel because none of the episodes have aired. The pilot – it was just phenomenal, really. I was shocked at the response. I think we all kind of were. We have to take it step-by-step because it's something really special and we all feel it. I hope people watch – every day has just been a blessing for us and we all really appreciate it.'

But FOX wasn't about to wait for word of mouth to spread the news: they were prepared to launch a big-budget marketing campaign of the highest order. Big, glossy print advertisements featuring key words from the reviews such as 'funny', 'original' and 'heartfelt' were ubiquitous in the big American cities. They positioned both print ads and *Glee*-ified street teams to best reach their principal audience – cheerleading camps, teen beach parties, summer music festivals and *American Idol* auditions.

Seeing all the big billboards was a pivotal moment for Dianna Agron (Quinn Fabray): 'My pinch-me moment came during the May UpFront in New York. You're staying in this beautiful hotel, seeing the huge billboards, giant balloons, *Glee* was everywhere in New York. I almost felt as if it was a dream.' But Dianna didn't realise that FOX's next move was perhaps the smartest thing of all: they were planning to show off *Glee*'s best asset: the cast.

First, there were in-depth panel discussions at conventions such as Comic-Con and Outfest. San Diego Comic-Con International (Comic-Con) is a massive four-day celebration of popular culture. It's the largest convention in the Western Hemisphere and over 140,000 people attended in 2009. Although it began in the 1970s with a focus on comic books, the event has now grown to be *the* destination for superfans to meet and greet with the cast and creators of their favourite programmes. The audience at Comic-Con 2009 got a sneak peek of *Glee*'s second episode, which sees Matthew Morrison (Will Schuester) rapping to Kanye West and Lea Michele (Rachel Berry) belting out Rihanna's '*Take a Bow*'. They also got to grill a panel from the cast, bombarding them with questions about what would come next, who was set to guest star and – even more importantly – how the fans could get involved. It was the cast's first taste of just how much love was out there for the show, even though only one episode had officially aired.

After Comic-Con, the young members of the cast – Cory Monteith, Lea Michele, Chris Colfer, Dianna Agron, Kevin McHale, Jenna Ushkowitz and Amber Riley – were sent on a cross-country tour to hit the malls of America. Called the 'Gleek! Tour', the idea was for the cast to interact with as many young teens as possible. The tour was held in Hot Topic clothing stores, who had manufactured special 'I'm a Gleek' T-shirts for the occasion. Besides signed T-shirts and posters, fans were treated to a long Q-and-A session where they could find out more about the hit show.

One TV critic blogged about her experience with the Gleek! Tour: 'When we showed up, the line to get in was pretty significant. If you can believe it, the cast thought there were going to be ten people there to see them, 20 tops. I guess it takes reading and writing about TV so often to understand how vast the hype is for a show, when these guys seemed to have no idea.'

FOX also gave the cast flip video cameras so they could film behind-the-scenes footage, interviews and more so that fans could continue to interact with the show throughout the summer, despite the season not beginning until September. To their great surprise, fans began to talk back, posting their own *Glee*-related videos. Dante Di Loreto, one of *Glee*'s executive producers, told the *Philadelphia Inquirer:* 'Right after we aired the pilot in May, people started posting their own versions of the songs performed in the show online. That's when we knew that we'd touched a chord. If we're doing it right then there's something for everyone. The relationships between the kids, the love stories and the friendships appeal to high-school kids, the more biting, acerbic comedy draws in the college students and parents watch it because they see the music they grew up with being reinvented. Different audiences see different things to love about it.'

Even more was happening behind the scenes and on the newest great advertising medium: the internet. FOX teamed up with Photobucket.com to host a competition to win a trip for two to the Teen Choice Awards. Users were invited to upload videos and photographs of themselves showing off their 'gold star potential', referencing the gold star Rachel Berry places at the end of every signature.

FOX was also beginning to realise the power of social networking sites such as Facebook and Twitter. Joe Earley hinted at what was to come: 'We'll be deepening engagements with characters from the show over the summer, working with social networks.'

Of course it helped that the majority of the cast was young and in tune with how Twitter worked before being encouraged by FOX to interact with fans even more. Dianna Agron shared her thoughts on Twitter and its importance on *AOL TV*: 'Well, I think that there's all this new technology and these people have been so gracious as to share with us what they enjoy, and so I think it's nice that if they would like to see what we're involved with and where we're going that they can kind of interact with us that way.'

Twitter gave fans the opportunity to pose questions to their favourite stars directly – and get real answers. It's a lot more intimate and immediate than writing a letter to an agent and hoping it might get passed on to the celebrity. Suddenly, the TV stars were accessible and fans were driven wild at just how friendly and open the cast were. These weren't distant and aloof actors on television: they were friends (be sure to check out a list of the *Glee* cast official twitters on page 281). Jenna Ushkowitz spoke to *Teen Daily* about Twitter: 'I don't think we realized how much of an effect social networking would have on our show. With a show like *Glee* that starts with a cult following, you have your hardcore fans whom we love very much, it's not only important for the show, but it's important to have the fans feel like they have an inside look into who we are along with our characters, and they can watch the show every week and tell us what they think and what they like. It's really important to be attached to your fans and to know what's being responded to and to share things with them. It makes us feel connected to them and it's really to know who they are. It's definitely helped our signings, it's definitely helped people be informed about coming out to our signings, and when *Glee* is on and why it's off the air for a few weeks. It's just an awesome, awesome way to stay connected and we're so lucky to have that outlet right now. I don't know what other TV shows did back then without it.'

GLEEFUL! MOMENT

Glee was the most twittered show of 2009, according to Trendrr, a website which tracks social media data. There were over 1.4 million tweets for *Glee*, versus 826,000 for the next most popular show, *American Idol*.

Actors having Twitter wasn't an inherently new concept – although *Glee*'s young cast certainly took it to the next level – but FOX did have plans for social media and *Glee* that were truly groundbreaking. So far, everything they had done had worked. The post-*Idol* airing of the pilot was genius, buzz had swarmed to immense levels over the summer thanks to great marketing, the previously unknown cast were fast becoming household names through their numerous tours and the proof was in the pudding: the Director's Cut of the pilot opened to fantastic ratings in September 2009. But FOX still wanted more: they were keen to give people a reason to watch reruns of the show and to do that, they coined a brand-new term: 'tweet-peats'.

Tweet-peats were repeats of the show featuring live messages from the official Twitter of the cast and producers broadcast along the bottom of the screen. *The Hollywood Reporter* wrote: 'During the episodes, viewers can follow Twitter-sent messages (online and on-air via a scroll near the bottom of the screen) providing commentary on the episodes, revealing behind-the-scenes details and answering fan questions.'

Admittedly, this new format didn't go down entirely well with some members of the audience, who found the scrolling 'tweets' too distracting. It didn't help that the commentary took up a good chunk of the bottom of the screen, obscuring much of the view. What it did mean, however, was that FOX had given audiences *three* reasons to watch the same episode of the same show – talk about a way to build hype. Even Ryan Murphy admitted the genius of it: 'By the time the series premières, that pilot will have been seen in three different versions, which I think is unheard-of in the history of TV.'

Clearly, FOX was throwing everything they had behind *Glee* to ensure its success. 'We have never taken our foot off the gas,' said Joe Earley in a dramatic understatement. Could it be that other networks were starting to get jumpy? It would certainly appear that way, as rival network NBC cancelled an appearance of the *Glee* cast on their annual *Macy's Thanksgiving Day Parade*. The action caused a stir of media publicity and *Glee*-mania grew ever stronger.

So strong, in fact, that the show became too big to contain solely in North America. *Glee* was taking off all over the world, not least down under in Australia, where the series was set to begin at the same time as in the US.

The cast were flown over to Australia to do a press tour. Most had never visited the country before and were totally unprepared for the experience awaiting them. *Glee* fever was well underway and fans were rabid. Cory Monteith, for one, was overwhelmed. 'Seriously, I have never in my life heard anyone scream like that,' he told the *Toronto Star*. 'I'm looking around at the others and going, "Hey, guys… this is, like, a whole other continent!"'

He had to get used to it quickly – the love, but also the Aussie slang! Radio and TV interviews with Cory and Lea often saw them confused by the presenters. One such presenter opened with: 'In the second episode, you pash each other…' 'We *what* in the *what*?' was Lea's reply. ('Pash' is Aussie slang for 'kiss', for the uninitiated!) Confusing lingo aside, over 2,000 Sydneysiders showed up for the cast appearance, so clearly they were somehow getting through. Lea summed it up by saying: 'In

Australia, the fans are incredibly enthusiastic and really passionate about the show. In the States we have some great fans, but not the type of hysteria we've experienced in Melbourne and Sydney.'

To be able to generate that kind of excitement a world away from the Hollywood studio they filmed in was unbelievable to the cast. But what was more unbelievable was that sometimes they didn't even need to visit the country for the hype to explode.

The explosion came in the form of the 'flash mob', perhaps the newest and most exciting form of viral marketing around today. A 'flash mob' occurs when a large group of people suddenly assemble in a public place, generally surprising ordinary passers-by. Although the *Glee*-related flash mobs are most likely the result of brilliant marketing by the television channels rather than generated by fans, they still served the same purpose. In Italy, a group of attractive Italian dancers invaded Rome's Galleria Alberto Sordi shopping mall. 'Don't Stop Believin'' began to blast out over the speakers and an elaborate choreographed dance began. The public reaction was amazing. Everyone stopped to watch the dancers (the main girl looked remarkably like Lea Michele) and soon they were bopping their heads and singing along to the music. A video of the event also went viral when it was put up on YouTube. Similar flash mobs took place in Tel Aviv's Dizengoff Centre and the entrance to Nachalat Binyamin market to promote the show in Israel. If that wasn't enough to get Europe excited for *Glee,* what else could they do?

The campaign in Japan was hugely elaborate as well. Two television advertisements featured retired sumo wrestling legend Akebono Taro singing 'Don't Stop Believin" were a great example of the sheer fun that *Glee* is all about. Despite being inherently a very American-centric concept (after all, there aren't very many Glee Clubs outside the American Midwest), the show clearly has universal appeal.

Alas, while the world was singing along to hit tunes from the show, the UK had to wait until late 2009 for its first-ever glimpse of *Glee.* In November 2009, *E4* ran the pilot to whet the appetite for the series beginning in early 2010. If anything, most of the UK reviews were even better than the ones in the US. 'Don't fight it,' said the *Daily Mail,* 'just give in and jump on the all-singing, all-dancing bandwagon.' Meanwhile, in the *Guardian,* self-professed Gleek Anna Pickard was effusive in her praise as she gave readers five reasons to watch *Glee*: '1. It's happy television, 2. It's not as much like *High School Musical* as you think it is, 3. It's sing-a-longable, 4. Jane Lynch, and 5. There's nothing else quite like it. It may be the middle of a miserable winter in the middle of miserable economic funk, but in a world of grey, *Glee* is a big bouncing bundle of joy.'

But of course with all the hype there were bound to be some detractors. The *Telegraph* wasn't immediately taken in, saying: 'This overhyped production is uninspired, confusing and with a simple plot to boot.' You can't please everyone!

The critics' response is all well and good, but it was the reaction of the viewers that *E4 really* cared about. And did they respond. *Glee* was the most-watched show on the multi-channel stations that night and garnered the highest audience for an acquired show on *E4* since an episode of *Lost* in August 2005.

Clearly, *Glee* mania had infected British viewers as well.

At the end of 2009, after an incredible, whirlwind year, several of the cast members posted their thoughts, hopes and wishes for the New Year on Twitter. Lea said: '@msleamichele: I can't say enough how wonderful this year was. I hope 2010 will be filled with just as much exciting and joyful things. Happy New Year!!!'

'@frankenteen: happy new year! 09 was nuts. looking forward to the next decade in a big way!' wrote Cory Monteith.

Now the trick will be for FOX and all its international counterparts to keep the hype going in new and innovative ways. Already the cast has spilled out into other shows, with Lea, Cory, Matthew Morrison and Chris Colfer appearing on the animated *Family Guy* spin-off, *The Cleveland Show.* 'It was awesome to do,'

Lea told *TV Guide* magazine. 'I'm a huge *Cleveland Show* fan and I've been literally stalking them to let me come on.'

The next stop for Gleeks is to be a musical tour in the summer of 2010. 'We're going to do what *American Idol* has done and put the kids on the road,' Ryan Murphy announced to *Digital Spy*. 'It all equals revenue streams for FOX.' Meanwhile, Cory announced the 2010 tour on his twitter: '@frankenteen: There is going to be a live #glee concert tour! in select cities; limited appearances. announcement and details soon. so excited!!!!' Needless to say, the tour will be huge!

So far we have seen Gleek tours and tweet-peats, terrific TV advertising campaigns and unique print ads. With rumours of a Broadway show, *Glee on Ice*, and a viewer sing-a-long all in the pipeline, one thing is clear: the possibilities are endless.

CHAPTER FOUR

HITTING THE HIGH NOTES

The magic of *Glee* is in the music. That's what makes it so special – so original – and it's the reason why people tune in, week after week.

And creator Ryan Murphy knew exactly what he *didn't* want *Glee* to be: he didn't want his characters simply to start singing as they walked down the street or in the middle of a normal conversation: 'I wanted to do a sort of postmodern musical. FOX was not interested, and neither was I, in doing a show where people burst into song.'

It's this grounding in reality that is part of *Glee*'s appeal. That's why Matthew Morrison (Will Schuester) believes the series works so much better than other attempted musical shows. 'This is a different approach,' he says. Of course, Murphy's song choices are still integrally linked to the emotion of the particular scene and the character, but there is also a reason to sing: a rehearsal, a performance or a fantasy sequence in the character's mind.

Already the creators had a model of a musical show that had worked phenomenally well: *American Idol*. 'We've learned some lessons about why that show works,' said Murphy. 'I think the key is to do songs that people know and interpret them in a different and unusual way.' Indeed, *Glee* has managed to take the *American Idol* model and become even more successful in the charts than its predecessor.

The genius behind the song selection is Murphy himself. It's one aspect that co-creators Ian Brennan and Brad Falchuk leave to him. Falchuk readily admits that his musical taste 'begins and ends with [Bruce Springsteen]', and while Brennan might make the odd recommendation, it's Murphy's taste that dominates. *Glee* is just lucky that taste is so wide-ranging. 'Ryan Murphy's brain is iTunes,' Lea Michele told the *Independent*. 'I've never met anyone with a music vocabulary as incredible as his. In the 13th episode, I go from singing a Barbra Streisand song into a Rolling Stones song into a Kelly Clarkson song.'

For Murphy, it's the biggest perk of being involved: 'The best part of my job is I pick all the songs, and people ask me how I do it, and it's just bizarre. I don't really know. Like, for instance, when we were doing the pilot, there was the sort of arch-nemesis group, the world's best show choir that's competing against our little ragtag group of losers called Vocal Adrenaline, and they're sort of like, you know, the neo-Nazis of show choir, that they train for 12 hours a day, and there really are groups like this. So it's not too much of a leap of faith.

'But I wanted them to do something that was sort of big and ironic, and then I was in my car, and I was listening to the Amy Winehouse album *Back to Black*, and "Rehab" came on, and I thought well, that's it because I think it would be funny for 16-year-olds to be singing about rehab and not really knowing what they're singing about, put through a prism of show choir.'

Murphy might have the final say, but that doesn't mean the cast won't try to influence his thoughts – by singing songs around him, they hope this becomes a form of subliminal messaging. 'We've learned how to hum or sing around the writers and around Ryan and make it their idea. Manipulate it so they think it was their idea – that they came up with it – then it'll totally make it in, but if you request it, it probably never will be,' revealed Jenna Ushkowitz. '"Bust Ya Windows" actually was Amber's favourite song and she had all of us listening to it. And then when we came back from the pilot, Ryan was, like, "guess what we're doing?" So she actually did get that.'

Choosing songs that the cast like has obviously been beneficial in helping them sing with the joy and passion associated with *Glee*. It definitely worked for 'Bust Ya Windows', as Amber's stirring version of the song is considered to be one of the best moments of the whole series so far.

But choosing songs is arguably the easy part. Murphy and the executives at FOX had no idea how musicians would respond to having their music reinterpreted in *Glee*. Music licensing fees have a reputation for being extremely expensive and it was down to music supervisor P.J. Bloom to clear the rights. Murphy may have found the perfect song for a scene, but if the artist didn't agree to share their work then they were out of luck. Bloom admits: 'We had this uphill battle of trying to licence some of the biggest songs in the world by the biggest artists in the world for an episodic musical that nobody had ever seen. And this type of show has failed miserably.' According to *Entertainment Weekly*, Bryan Adams and Coldplay are two such artists to have said no – at least, for now – to *Glee* using their music.

The majority of artists are able to see the bigger picture – and the potential that *Glee* has to boost their profiles. 'I was obsessed with *Grease* as a kid. I was obsessed with Journey. I was obsessed with Aretha Franklin. So when we wrote the pilot, we wrote those songs in. Then in the process of getting them cleared, we were shocked that after a lot of these big artists and their companies read the script, they approved it.

'I think the key to it is they loved the tone of it. They loved that this show was about optimism and young kids, for the most part, reinterpreting their classics for a new audience,' Murphy explained.

In retrospect, he can make the whole process sound effortless but it most definitely wasn't. Can you imagine *Glee* without the signature track 'Don't Stop Believin''? Well, it almost didn't happen. '[We] were battling [writer/ex-vocalist] Steve Perry's concerns about how his music is exploited,' recalled P.J. Bloom. '[We] were battling the band's inner turmoil. It took everyone's efforts – mine, [FOX executive in charge of music] Geoff Bywater, all the publicity people, the promo people – to develop an overall campaign to convince Steve Perry and the band to be involved.' However, Perry is no stranger to having his song licenced to a TV show – during the series finale of the final season of *The Sopranos*, 'Don't Stop Believin'' was playing. He was hesitant then, too, but approve he finally did, and 'Don't Stop Believin'' has gone on to become a renewed chart hit for Journey and for *Glee*.

The musicians' approval, combined with the willingness of FOX to pay to licence music from the biggest artists in the business, meant Murphy had an almost 100 per cent success rate in getting the songs he wanted – and sometimes at a discount: 'FOX has really been supportive in giving us resources and manpower to mount these big numbers. And the music community has really embraced us. "Take a Bow" is something that would usually go for hundreds of thousands of dollars, and we got it for a really good price. And we have other artists saying, "Hey, take this for free."'

This is a bit misleading – let's be clear, the music industry is no charity. Quite the opposite, in fact – it's all about business, *big* business. Artists and their labels were excited to see their music reinterpreted as this has the potential to breathe new life into the original tracks. The proof came later in the chart sales after each *Glee* episode: Rihanna's 'Take a Bow' saw a 189 per cent boost while Usher's 'Confessions Pt. II' had a 221 per cent increase in sales after both songs featured on the show. Those numbers are hard to argue with, and success breeds success. Today more artists are eager to have their songs featured on the show. Billy Joel even called up Ryan Murphy and told him, 'I love the show. Please use my music.'

Of course, the flip side to this was the opportunity for a forward-thinking record company to sell the cast's versions of the songs as singles. FOX knew this could be a particularly lucrative contract and so they arranged a meeting with all the head honchos of the major record companies. They played a sample four-minute trailer from the pilot episode and explained the concept of the show. The record executives loved it, and there was plenty of competition. Eventually it was Rob Stringer at Columbia Records who convinced the FOX team that he was the right man for the job. 'Everyone else said, "Oh, this could do really well," but Rob said, "I don't think you know what you have,"' Murphy told *Billboard*. 'He always had a plan and a passion.'

'I'm not sure other labels saw it as dramatically as we did,' said Stringer. 'People saw the show and loved it, but because the songs were cover versions, I think they honestly didn't think that the potential for the music was as great as we thought it was.' He was quick to assemble a team at Columbia to focus on promoting *Glee*, who would work closely with FOX. The label's plan was to release the strongest songs from the episodes about two weeks *before* a particular episode was set to air. Those same songs were then chosen for use in the television advertisements for upcoming episodes. 'It's all coming back to us as additional marketing,' said FOX senior VP of marketing, Laurel Bernard. 'The show pushes the music, and the music equally pushes the show.'

It still goes without saying that without the right arrangement for the cast, the cover versions of the songs wouldn't have a shelf life. That's why Murphy was prepared to bring in the best team to help make his musical vision a reality. P.J. Bloom, the aforementioned music supervisor, was the leader of this team. Previously, he had worked as the music supervisor on Murphy's *Nip/Tuck*. But that was just the tip of the iceberg of Bloom's experience, which extended to over 50 films and hundreds of TV shows, commercials, video games and theme parks. He was even responsible for updating the music on the Disney theme park ride 'Space Mountain'.

It's hard to imagine now, but Bloom was not entirely convinced by *Glee* when Murphy first came to him. In *Variety*, he explained his hesitation: 'Ryan said, "We're going to do an episodic musical on show choir." I said, "Jeez, I'm really not all that familiar with what show choir is." So he sat me down in front of his computer and went on YouTube and started pulling up the video on show choirs from around the country, doing pop songs, classic songs. I had really never seen anything like it, and in all honesty I wasn't sure whether it was the greatest thing I'd ever seen or the worst thing I'd ever seen.'

Murphy eventually won him over and Bloom, an enthusiastic advocate of the show ever since, has managed to win contracts from notoriously protective artists like Yoko Ono and Neil Diamond. 'It was very difficult to convince Yoko Ono that it was the right thing to do,' revealed Bloom, on trying to licence the John Lennon classic 'Imagine'. 'She needed to truly understand how the music was going to be used. The added component of us wanting to have a deaf choir signing the song made for this incredibly poignant moment. It really took a lot of convincing to get her on board and realise that it was a great, great moment, and a tribute to John and his song.'

Using Neil Diamond's 'Sweet Caroline' was almost the worst disaster – despite being one of the show's sweetest moments. Bloom had to do some fast talking as Diamond retracted the clearance for the song after it had already been shot. He told *Variety*, 'had they stuck to their position, it would have been an absolute disaster on multiple levels. But I was able to get it turned back around.'

All's well that ends well, and Neil Diamond loved the rendition. He even took to his official Twitter to voice his pleasure. @NeilDiamond wrote on 22 October 2009: 'Hey, so who's this guy Puck singing "Sweet Caroline" so good,so good,so good on #Glee? Loved it!!' He was then happy to allow the *Glee* team to use whatever song of his they wanted on the show.

Despite momentary setbacks, the music selection was coming together far more easily than Murphy had anticipated. But once a song was chosen and Bloom had cleared the rights, it needed to be arranged for the cast. This challenge was presented to Swedish-born music producer and songwriter, Adam Anders.

Already Anders had experienced a great deal of success in the music industry. He wrote songs for the boy band Backstreet Boys and was involved in TV shows like *Hannah Montana* and the hit movie, *High School Musical*. Yet nothing came close to the challenge that Ryan Murphy now presented him with. Not only was he to arrange songs that often only had one vocal part to suddenly suit twelve singers, but he would also be responsible for the amazing 'mash-ups' that feature in so many of the episodes. Some of the mash-ups include Bon Jovi's 'It's My Life' mixed with Usher's 'Confessions Part II,' and then another of Beyoncé's 'Halo' with Katrina & The Waves' 'Walking on Sunshine'. Anders explained some of his methods to *FOX LA*: 'The main thing is that I want to stay true to the original song... a lot of the time we reinterpret some of the instruments as vocals.

'Some of the mash-ups we've done, the songs do not belong together. I'm like, dude you're crazy for trying this but it works out and it's a really great challenge,' Anders admitted. Through the power of Skype and the internet, he collaborates with a partner across the ocean in Sweden to come up with some of the most innovative music arrangements on television.

Anders gets a little help from home, too. When he needs to pre-record a 'guide' for the cast so they know what to sing and how the song has been arranged, he enlists his wife, fellow accomplished-musician Nikki Hassman-Anders, to sing the female guide, while he sings the male. The process can take weeks and with Murphy pushing for even more songs per episode, Anders will have his work cut out in the future.

Once the song is arranged, it's down to choreographer extraordinaire Zach Woodlee to dream up some funky moves. An experienced backing dancer (he danced for Mandy Moore and Madonna on their world tours), his big choreographing break came when he started work on *Hairspray*, the movie. You can also spot him as the dance instructor on the 'learn the steps' section of the *Hairspray* DVD.

Murphy encourages Woodlee to push the actors to their limits. The iconic 'Don't Stop Believin'' scene took 75 takes to shoot. Another great example of Woodlee pushing the cast to their limit is during the episode 'Wheels', when he had to choreograph a dance move with all the cast in wheelchairs. Murphy wanted to make sure they never left their chairs during that particular number: 'Artie doesn't get to get up ever, so I didn't want anyone to get up.'

Woodlee was happy to take up the challenge. 'If it looked too fun and easy, it wouldn't read right... Ryan really wanted people to understand what Artie deals with.'

Between choreography, arrangements and rights clearing, *Glee* is more expensive to produce than your average show, but FOX were very understanding and wanted the series to succeed in every way. Geoff

Bywater, FOX's executive VP of music, explained: 'In *24* you would have the special effects budget – in *Glee* you have a music budget. Music is our special effects.'

And all the extra hard work really began to pay off when the chart positions and iTunes sales came rolling in. The first week after the pilot aired on 9 September 2009, the *Glee* version of 'Don't Stop Believin'' had sold 177,000 downloads, according to Nielsen SoundScan, and entered the Billboard Hot 100 at No. 4 – which is higher than the Journey original ever charted. A month after the pilot aired, the week ending 18 October, it had sold 522,000 downloads.

'In all the years that I've been in the business, I've never worked on anything quite like this,' observed Geoff Bywater. 'It's a real cultural phenomenon that you can just feel. We've got people who are going to have great acting careers and recording histories for themselves in the future.' By the end of the first half of season one, 46 singles released by the *Glee* cast were available for download on iTunes. Collectively, they have amassed 4.2 million downloads and counting. Twenty-five of the tracks went on to hit the Billboard 100, with 'Don't Stop Believin'' reaching the highest position of No. 4. As the music is available exclusively on iTunes before other outlets, 17 of the tracks have made the Top 25 iTunes downloads chart. Those tracks, with the chart positions, are listed here:

'Don't Stop Believin'' (No. 1)

'Somebody To Love' (No. 3)

'Alone' (No. 8)

'My Life Would Suck Without You' (No. 9)

'It's My Life/Confession Pt II' (No. 9)

'Take a Bow' (No. 11)

'Sweet Caroline' (No. 11)

'Keep Holding On' (No. 12)

'Halo'/'Walking On Sunshine' (No. 12)

'Don't Rain On My Parade' (No. 13)

'Last Christmas' (No. 14 on Top 25, No. 1
   in holiday songs)

'Maybe This Time' (No. 15)

'You Can't Always Get What You Want' (No. 15)

'Defying Gravity' (Cast Version) (No. 16)

'Smile' (Cover of Charlie Chaplin Song) (No. 20)

'I'll Stand By You' (No. 21)

'Endless Love' (No. 24)

Columbia Records were shocked at just how quickly their deal with FOX was paying off. 'We knew that once the show started rolling, it would be great,' admitted Rob Stringer, 'But to be honest, I didn't think it would be this big this quickly. I thought it would take people a moment to catch up, but the reaction has been instant.'

The only sensible thing after the immediate success of the singles was to release an album. On 3 November

2009, *Glee: The Music, Volume 1* was released in the US. It contained 17 of the most popular tracks from the first half of the opening 13 episodes and sold over 677,000 copies at the last count and rose to No. 27 on the Billboard Top 200 Album chart. This was quickly followed by *Glee: The Music, Volume 2* on 8 December 2009, which sold over 500,000 copies since its release and reached No. 22 on the chart. In January 2010 both albums certified gold in the US by the Recording Industry Association of America (RIAA) for selling over 500,000 units each.

The albums would help reach to those consumers who perhaps weren't yet the type to go online to buy their music from iTunes. 'We think there will be a huge population of passive buyers walking through stores during the holidays and saying, "Oh, I've seen *Glee*,' and picking up the record,' said Bywater, 'I think we'll see considerable sales in the Walmarts, Targets and Best Buys of the world.'

Both albums, however, had mixed critical reviews because of the varying abilities of the cast members. Few had anything bad to say about Lea Michele, Amber Riley or Matthew Morrison, but Dianna Agron and Cory Monteith were two of the actors generally singled out for having weaker voices. 'Not all *Glee* members are created equal,' wrote *AllMusic*. 'Cory Monteith (the show's hunky football captain) and Dianna Agron (the alternately caustic and vulnerable head cheerleader) can't sing nearly as well as their co-stars – but this soundtrack has enough star power to keep things trucking along, especially when powerhouse alto Lea Michele takes the wheel.' Hardly a surprise especially when you consider Dianna and Cory's lack of experience before joining *Glee*.

They may have weakened the album from the critics' point of view, but the strength of the show lay in having an emotional story and context within which to ground each of the song choices. 'If you have seen the show and love it, you will want this to prompt those happy memories,' remarked Bill Lamb on About.com. *Rolling Stone* magazine wrote: 'Star Matthew Morrison couldn't rap his way out of a 98° rehearsal. But Amber "Mercedes" Riley crushes Jazmine Sullivan's "Bust Your Windows," and the Gleeks' "Don't Stop Believin'" is a triumphal moment against which resistance is futile.'

Resistance indeed was futile. Some critics were surprised by their own love for the music, which could sometimes come across as professionally recorded karaoke. *Entertainment Weekly* wrote: 'Much like the TV show itself, there is so much about this soundtrack that shouldn't work. Sickly-sweet vocals. Theme-park-level arrangements. Cheesy song choices ("True Colors", "Lean on Me") that get even cheesier without the onscreen enthusiasm of the cast as a distraction. And yet it *does* work.'

And it worked all over the world. Once *Glee*-mania spread outside the US, there was no stopping it. The singles hit the charts in Canada, Australia, New Zealand, Ireland and the UK. In fact, *Glee* hit its highest chart position yet when the cast version of 'Don't Stop Believin'' went to No. 2 in the UK Singles chart.

According to *BBC News*, five *Glee* singles broke the UK Top 75 Singles Chart within a week of the show's debut on *E4*. 'Don't Stop Believin'' initially debuted at No. 5, with the covers of Rihanna's 'Take a Bow' at 43, Kanye West's 'Gold Digger' at 49, Amy Winehouse's 'Rehab' at 62 and 'On My Own' from *Les Misérables* at No. 73. This was an incredible success for a show that had only just crossed over the Atlantic that week.

All round, it's an amazing achievement for a show that hasn't even completed its first season. '*Glee* isn't even anywhere near where it will be in a month or year's time,' says Rob Stringer. 'The show will be five times bigger than it is now, just from word-of-mouth, so we're not in any panic or rush to overplay things because there's plenty of time.' With many of the cast signed up to create their own solo albums, *Glee* is set to dominate the charts for years to come, too.

CHAPTER FIVE

ON-SET SHENANIGANS

With such a young ensemble cast, the atmosphere on set is electric. Filmed predominantly at the Paramount Studios lot in Hollywood, California, the cast spend hours learning, rehearsing and finally performing the elaborate numbers and filming the show together. Everyone is so insistent they are friends that it's hard not to believe them. 'The atmosphere on the set is crazy-fun,' Lea Michele (Rachel Berry) gushed on-air in Australia. 'We're like wild kids. We have so much together... we all just got really lucky that we vibed so well together. We clicked.'

'We're best friends. We're one happy family,' Jenna Ushkowitz (Tina Cohen-Chang) told *Seventeen* magazine. 'I think for the most part [the chemistry] was pretty instant,' said Naya Rivera, who plays Cheerio Santana Lopez. 'We're a really big cast. We have twelve *Glee* members now, our teacher and a couple other adults. Within the Glee Club itself, we hang out all the time and it is like going to work and just hanging out with your friends all day. On the set, there is always someone to hang out with or talk to. It's great! Everyone really does love everyone else.' Whether it's piling into someone's trailer to watch *The Breakfast Club* for the umpteenth time or pulling pranks on their co-workers, the cast of *Glee* are always together.

Lea explained her close relationship with other cast members to *New York* magazine: 'The *Glee* kids, they're my family in L.A. Each one I go to for a different thing. Amber [Riley, who plays Mercedes, the sassy black girl], she's my tough love. Chris Colfer [who plays Kurt, the fey kid with amazing vocal range] will make me laugh, like, any day. I love him to death. He's also great if you're having a bad day and you want to cry over two pints of ice cream while watching *Madea Goes to Jail*. Yes, we've done it, and it was the greatest night of my life. Jenna Ushkowitz, who plays Tina [the Goth Asian stutterer], was in *Spring Awakening*, and I've known her since I'm 8 years old and she's my soul sister. I live with Dianna [Agron, who plays celibate cheerleader Quinn and Rachel's arch-nemesis]. Cory Monteith [who plays Finn, the hunky football player with a heart and killer pipes] is hysterical, and my technology guru. The poor guy, it's constant with me. "Oh my God, the cover fell off my phone. I don't know how to put it back on." Like, all the time.'

You would be forgiven for thinking that some of the cast mates must surely need the occasional break from each other. Yet the cast genuinely seem happy to hang out with each other all the time. The younger members even have their own area of the set where they can chill and relax, either in between takes or while they're waiting for a shot to be set up. 'We set up chairs and fake palm trees, and have a sign that says, "Club Cast,"' Cory Monteith told *OK! Magazine*. 'We sit around and sing songs – that's how some of the songs featured on the show have been written in.'

They also play a lot of games in 'Club Cast', one of their favourites being 'Mafia'. Sometimes known as 'Assassin' or 'Werewolf', 'Mafia' is a game best played in groups, where one or more players is assigned a position in the Mafia, one is a detective and the rest are innocent villagers. The aim is for the detective to find and identify all the Mafia members before the villagers get killed. 'We play Mafia a lot,' Kevin McHale (Artie Abrams) admitted in a television interview. 'One of the PAs on set is a genius at Mafia. We got everyone into it.'

Sometimes they ended up having so much fun on set that they forgot the show, with the exception of the pilot, hadn't actually been seen by anyone yet. This was all in the nerve-wracking days when they weren't even sure if they would get to finish filming the first whole season, let alone dreaming beyond that. However, on set there was an air of confidence that they had something special and audiences *were* going to get it. That confidence – along with hours of working hard to make it a reality – created a sense of comfort in the actors, although they could never have predicted just how successful the show would become. 'We were completely separated from the rest of the world while filming,' recalled Kevin McHale. 'We worked crazy hours filming all 13 [episodes] back-to-back and we forgot that people were actually going to watch them. We always talked about what it would be like if this happened, or if that happened, but it's even greater to see how it's worked out. We all feel so lucky to be a part of this amazing show that people truly love.'

It didn't end in the studio, though: the cast even hang out off set. 'We have Gleekends when we bowl, we have sleepovers, and three of us actually live in the same apartment complex, so it's a little like a college dorm,' admits Jenna. 'I think the off screen is what reflects to the chemistry on screen and I think that's why it works. It really is not something that you can learn or teach, I think it's just there, and we're lucky enough to have it. Especially being outcasts, I think on the show the reflection that we are the underdog and we are the ones that people will root for because we're not as "cool," I think that also bonded us as well to make us feel like we all are actually a unit.'

There have been some incredible bonding moments throughout the show's filming. One of *Glee*'s most poignant episodes, when the fictional Haverbrook School for the Deaf performs 'Imagine' in sign language, really brought the cast and crew together. 'I mean, the cameramen, the entire crew and the cast were in tears. That was such an incredible day,' said Jenna.

It was Lea who had a radical idea: what about a tattoo to commemorate the experience? 'We were all quite tired, had a bit of wine and I managed to convince two of the cast members to go out and get tattoos. So we all have little tattoos on our feet now. It says, "Imagine". It made a lot of sense that night.' Jenna, along with Kevin McHale, was one of the cast members who went with Lea to get the tattoo, although hers is written in script along her forearm: 'A bunch of us actually got "Imagine" tattoos afterwards because it was such a nice checkpoint in our lives.'

It's not all sweetness and light and Kumbaya-sing-a-longs on set, though! The actors love to play pranks on each other as well. It's also hardly surprising that Mark Salling (who plays bad-boy jock Puck) and Cory Monteith are often behind the gags. 'We were doing a scene in the last episode where the auditorium was filled. They use extras as well as these dummies that they put in chairs, [laughs] so we'd go around putting the dummies in people's trailers. We'd stack them so they'd be against the door so when they opened the trailer door, they'd fall on them. [laughs] It would just scare the hell out of people. That was a lot of fun,' said Mark to AfterElton.com. Not to be outdone, Cory told *OK! Magazine*, 'One time I put a banana in [executive producer] Dante Di Loreto's tailpipe. He drove off and it exploded his muffler.'

The boys aren't the only ones in on the fun, though. Jenna and Amber pulled a prank on Josh Sussman, who plays Jacob Ben Israel – a nerdy character with a big thing for Rachel Berry. 'Amber decided to leave one of our guest stars a note that said, "I can't wait for our scene!" with big lip marks, "Love, Lea Michele" and so he went up to Lea and was, like, "I'm very excited for our scene together, thank you for your note" and she was, like, "What? What note?" and me and Amber are in the make-up chair, shaking and convulsing,' Jenna revealed.

So it's obvious that the young cast gets along really well, but how do the adults fit in? 'I am the old person on the set,' said Jane Lynch. 'Within two minutes of being on *Glee*, I became the "seasoned veteran" – I don't know how that happened because I was the young upstart just yesterday.' Lynch might not be the young upstart any more, but she has relished the opportunity to be the 'mum' on set. She even referred to the cast as 'my babies' when they visited her backstage at her off-Broadway play, *Love, Loss, and What I Wore*. Because her role did not require as much dancing or, at that point, no singing, she was only on set for two or three days a week as opposed to five for the rest of the cast.

Matthew Morrison, on the other hand, is always on set. He likes to keep the kids in check – even if he doesn't feel that far away from them in age, they still see him as a mentor figure. 'They all look up to me, and I can kind of tell them what to do, telling them to shut up and go to work,' he said to *New York* magazine. 'They're always having fun and being loud.'

And they needed to let off steam after performing. Heather Morris explained their schedule to the *Buffalo Examiner*: 'It varies. Sometimes it will be like 5 am to 2 am, but not often. Sometimes it will be like 12 pm to 2 pm.' Maintaining the same energy levels must be really hard, even for the most seasoned member of the cast. And as one of Beyoncé's former backing dancers, Heather certainly knows the meaning of hard work: 'The hardest part is probably exerting all that energy, all day long for, like, 18 hours straight, that might be the hardest part. You have to sit and wait while they set up shots. It's not hard because you love it, but it's also really tiring.'

Still, the dedication of working until 3am often paid

off. For Naya Rivera, practising so hard helped her to feel more prepared to sing Aretha Franklin's 'Say A Little Prayer' – her first real performance on the show: 'I would probably say my most memorable moment is when the three cheerleaders performed a little number as an audition number. I hadn't danced in such a long time and I was really nervous. I practised until 3:30am to get it right. I went there the next day, we did it and we did such a good job. The people from *Nip/Tuck* actually came over because we're on the set next to them. They came over, they were watching and they were clapping. It was weird, but oddly uplifting for work to be put in that situation. I felt like I accomplished something.'

If performing gave the cast such a buzz, it was nothing compared to their feelings of elation when praise and support for the show began to pour in. All those nights of hard work were finally beginning to pay off. Suddenly, it wasn't the *Glee* cast against the world, but the whole world wanting to join in with the group, who were clearly having so much fun. Going on a tour of the malls of America and then to Australia really brought them together, as did seeing the roll out from FOX's massive marketing campaign. 'I think the night we saw the first commercial had to be the most memorable for me,' said Amber. 'It was the first time it felt real.'

When it was announced that *Glee* was coming back to film a second season, the cast were elated – they had already spent a year having the greatest time in the world and finally they had been given the green light to continue. It's as if the positivity and happiness that they feel behind the scenes is strong enough to transfer through the cameras, through the television screens and into people's homes. Heather Morris tried to get her head around the fact that they had become a worldwide phenomenon: 'You can't explain it – it relates to every single person in the entire world. And we're such a positive group. We're always so close, everyone – from the lighting crew, production, everybody behind the show, craft services, we're all close to them. I don't know, it's like the energy that's there just reaches out to everybody else, that's probably why.'

CHAPTER SIX
THE SHOW MUST GO ON

Watch out, spoilers ahead!

So what's coming up for *Glee*? In the US, the rest of the first season airs on 13 April 2010, to be swiftly followed by networks around the world. All through the winter/spring hiatus, while the first episodes of *Glee* were airing in the UK, Gleeks everywhere anxiously snapped up any piece of information they could find regarding the last nine episodes and what they could look forward to in Season 2. Fortunately, the cast were just as eager to discover where their storylines were going and were happy to share tidbits with the fans! 'We just read the new script,' said Jenna Ushkowitz. 'It's like Christmas! It's gonna be a great one so we are very excited. I think it's gonna be edgier and riskier, and we are just really excited to get back to work.' Dianna Agron's comments echoed that same excitement: 'I've read the first three episodes and they're so delicious, amazing and I think that everybody will be really, *really* happy where all the characters are headed.' One thing is for sure – the episodes are going to be bigger and better than ever, with an average of eight or nine numbers each, up from the previous five to six.

The big rumour that sent the Gleek community into speculation overdrive was the announcement of a 'Madonna' episode. Ryan Murphy wrote to the Queen of Pop, saying, 'We really want to do a tribute to you.' She in turn accepted willingly and allowed the show access to her entire catalogue. Kevin McHale voiced some of the disbelief the cast felt on hearing of Madonna's approval: 'The fact that Madonna has even heard of *Glee* is kind of ridiculous! I'm hoping she wanders by our set one day and goes, "Oh, they're shooting? Let me go say hi!" But I'm so excited to see what songs they pick because I know they won't just use the hits. That's not what they do.' In fact, Murphy and co. have already used one Madonna song when Quinn sings 'Papa Don't Preach' in Episode 11, 'Hairography'. But upcoming is a full-on, all-Material Girl extravaganza. 'It's big... Huge,' Murphy told *Entertainment Weekly*. 'We're shooting it now. It's got like ten numbers in it, and the production value is very big.'

Those ten numbers were leaked by MadonnaTribe.com and the show is set to include these tracks: 'Borderline', 'Open Your Heart', 'Burning Up', '4 Minutes', 'Crazy For You', 'Like A Virgin', 'Like A Prayer', 'What It Feels Like For A Girl', 'Vogue' and 'Express Yourself', with six of the tracks being sung by Lea Michele. According to MadonnaTribe.com: '"Borderline" and "Open Your Heart" are actually mixed into one song as sort of a medley while all the other songs are performed in full or in an edit version. All songs' arrangements are inspired by the album original versions of the songs except for "Express Yourself", inspired by the famous "Video Version" and "Crazy For You" which is presented as an exclusive acoustic guitar version.'

This particular episode will also feature some of the actors who haven't had much singing to do so far. The most highly anticipated of these is Jane Lynch, who is confirmed to be singing 'Vogue'. 'I'm having a lot of fittings for this Madonna video we're doing,' said Jane. 'We're basically doing it frame for frame.' Expect therefore to see Jane fitted out in one of Madonna's famous conical-shaped bras designed by Jean Paul Gaultier because 'You're going to find out that Sue [Sylvester] wants to get a makeover.' And although it hasn't officially been confirmed, there are strong rumours that Jayma Mays, who plays Emma Pillsbury, will get to sing 'Like A Virgin'. Jayma told *TV Guide* that the song she sings is 'very appropriate and fitting for my character', and also that, 'If they said my character's a virgin, I wouldn't be surprised.'

Whatever happens, it's already the most highly anticipated episode of the last nine. Of course, there's always a danger that with all the hype that has grown up around it, fans will be underwhelmed by the actual broadcast. Lea Michele tells us not to worry: 'I think the fans will not be disappointed in the Madonna episode. It's big and it's powerful, and the characters who are interacting together are not the ones you would expect. I feel like with each episode everything keeps escalating to a new level.' Ryan Murphy has also revealed that he's going to be very respectful of Madonna's catalogue: 'We adore her and worship her, so when I'm directing, I'm always like, "Do it for Madonna."'

Murphy looks prepared to try plenty of new things in the last nine, and by riding the wave of success from the first thirteen episodes he is able to take a lot more risks and move the show into fun and innovative new directions. Since all the previous songs have been cover versions, the next logical route to take is original numbers. 'I've had a lot of calls from songwriters, to the point where it's kind of embarrassing and ridiculous,' Murphy told *Billboard* magazine. 'So we're writing an episode called "Original Song", where the teacher asks the kids to write their own piece of music.'

With a pick of songwriters at his disposal, Murphy went straight to the top and confirmed that Diane Warren was to write two of the big ballads for the episode. And he couldn't have chosen a more perfect songwriter to do *Glee* justice. Warren is responsible for such mega-hits as 'I Don't Want to Miss a Thing' by Aerosmith, Celine Dion's 'Because You Loved Me' and 'Unbreak My Heart' by Toni Braxton. In 2009, she also collaborated with Andrew Lloyd Webber to write the UK's entry for the Eurovision Song Contest, 'It's My Time' sung by the newest Sugababe, Jade Ewen. Diane Warren is widely considered to be a song-writing genius and her collaborations with *Glee* are bound to be incredibly exciting.

Another songwriter who has announced he is writing for *Glee* is OneRepublic's Ryan Tedder. Along with the smash hit 'Apologize', he co-wrote 'Bleeding Love' by Leona Lewis and 'Halo' by Beyoncé. When asked by Idolator.com about the mash-up in Episode 6 ('Vitamin D') of 'Halo' and 'Walking On Sunshine', Tedder admitted that he was delighted with the outcome. '*Glee* is actually my new addiction,' he continued. 'I download every episode. They actually just approached me: Adam Anders, the guy who does all the music, approached me about two weeks ago to do original music for the next season. So I'm gonna be doing at least one song for the next season that's original.'

Ryan Murphy might love to bring in successful songwriters and feature A-list guest stars (check out Guest Stars Galore! on page 175 to find out more about who's coming to *Glee*) but his absolute favourite part of the job is still discovering new talent and bringing it to the forefront. Naturally, the *Glee*-world went mad when he announced that the team would be conducting a nationwide search throughout the US for three new cast members – a casting call that would be open to professionals and amateurs alike. *Glee*-wannabes could upload video auditions of themselves in the hope of being spotted by the casting team.

He also revealed the roles that the three new actors would be taking on in the second season, which sparked a lot of discussion itself. They were searching for a boyfriend for Kurt, a rival for Rachel and a male version of Mercedes. Kurt's boyfriend is rumoured to be on the football team. Murphy confirmed, 'We're going to make them a power couple. We're not going to do the whole hiding in the shadows thing: we're going to make them popular, and out and proud and glamorous, like prom king and king. We're doing the *opposite* of what's been done.' He also revealed some more details on Rachel's rival: 'We're casting sort of an Eve Harrington to kind of steal Rachel's thunder a little.' Eve Harrington is a character from the 1950 American movie *All About Eve,* who befriends a famous-but-ageing Broadway actress Margo Channing (Bette Davis) by claiming to be her biggest fan. In taking advantage of Margo's generous offer of a job as her assistant, Eve (Anne Baxter) cunningly schemes to steal the lead role in a hit musical from Margo – and succeeds. Could we see a young admirer plotting to steal Rachel Berry's thunder? She's not going to have an easy time wrenching the spotlight away from Rachel, that's for sure!

'The third role is an R&B-singing teen,' Murphy confirmed to Ausiello of the Ausiello Files on *Entertainment Tonight*. He would act as a male counterpart to Mercedes, and there was also a hint that there might be a spark of love interest between the two characters.

What else can we expect from the next episodes? Murphy plans to revive the Puck and Rachel storyline: 'We just finished [writing] a special episode where they are together, and they have two numbers together. It's Episode 4 [of the last nine], "Bad Reputation."' A behind-the-scenes video posted by Cory Monteith also showed Amber Riley and Chris Colfer dressed up in Cheerios uniforms while dancing. Could the two characters be joining the Cheerios? That would be unexpected!

The important thing to remember is that Murphy and his creative team are always reworking the show right up to the very last minute. They have already demonstrated a willingness to play around with character relationships if they don't work and to add in new songs as they see fit. Who knows what surprises we Gleeks have in store, but rest assured, it's going to be great!

THE CAST

CHAPTER SEVEN
ONCE MORE, FROM THE TOP!

On set, Matthew Morrison is known as *triple threat*. 'But you have to say it with a high-pitched voice: "Triple threat,"' he says, laughing. 'Yep. That's what they call me around here.'

The nickname won't come as any surprise to the millions of Gleeks who tune in to watch Matthew Morrison sing, dance and act as the idealistic high-school Spanish teacher Will Schuester (or Mr. Schuester to the kids). Matthew's easy charm and old-fashioned Hollywood good looks make it hard to imagine anyone else in the role but for the show's producers, finding the perfect 'Mr. Schuester' was a lot harder than it seemed. Brad Falchuk, one of *Glee*'s co-creators and an executive producer, told *Emmy* magazine: 'You'd think there must be a lot of good-looking thirty-year-old guys who can sing, dance and act, but there really aren't.' Enter Matthew, a relative unknown in the TV world, who was poised to break onto the small screen in a big way.

Matthew Morrison was born on 30 October 1978 in Fort Ord, a military base in northern California. His parents both worked in the medical field: his mother was an RN and his dad worked as a midwife. Being an only child and a self-proclaimed 'army brat', Matthew was often forced to make his own entertainment – something he credits with making him a better actor: '[My parents] were working all the time. I had this wild imagination, and I'd come home after school and stage these whole scenes with my toy knights.'

Early on in his life, Matthew's family moved down to sunny Orange County, California. But that wasn't where he initially picked up the acting bug. Instead, it was a visit to his extended family in Arizona that awakened the passion. His aunt and uncle 'didn't really want to deal with me, so they threw me and my cousin into this children's theatre, and I just had a ball. And I said I wanted to do [acting] after that.'

This was no fleeting childhood dream. Matthew's determination to become an actor from a young age shone through as he auditioned (and won) a place at the prestigious Orange County High School of the Arts (OCHSA). On its website, OCHSA says that it provides 'a creative, challenging, and nurturing environment that offers bright and talented students unparalleled preparation for higher education and a profession in the arts.' Other notable alumni include teen star Vanessa Hudgens of *High School Musical* fame and Ashley Benson from *The O.C.*

Matthew fondly looks back on his time in high school. He says that he was always *that guy* in school: 'I was president of my class, played the lead in every school play, was prom king, on the soccer team.'

In fact, he was so good at soccer that he considered training full-time for the American National side in preparation for the Olympics but his love of performing refused to be pushed out of the spotlight: 'There was a turning point. In my sophomore year of high school I had to choose between soccer or singing: I think I chose the right one, but it was probably one of the hardest decisions I've ever had to make.'

Perhaps that's why the *Glee* character that Matthew feels he relates to most is not the teacher, but high-school quarterback Finn Hudson, who also rides the line between a love of sport and a passion for singing. His time at OCHSA did inspire the character of Will Schuester in a different way, however. He speaks extremely highly of Ralph Opacic, the founder and executive director of his alma mater: 'He's the motivator... always optimistic, never quitting.'

As for the founder himself, he is honoured to have played a part in forming what is now one of the most popular characters on TV. 'I'm so proud of [Matthew],' he told *Star* magazine.

In fact, nothing could live up to Matthew's experience at OCHSA. After graduating in 1997, he decided to move eastward to New York where he had secured a place with NYU's Tisch School of the Arts – whose alumni include megawatt names like Woody Allen, Angelina Jolie and Martin Scorsese, among numerous others. But after a period of frustration at the college, where he began to realise that perhaps OCHSA had already taught him all he needed to know about performing, combined with the Tisch rule that students couldn't audition for roles during their first two years at NYU, he dropped out and landed a role in the Broadway production of *Footloose*.

A year later, in 2000, he joined the boy band LMNT (pronounced 'element'), but quickly began to realise that the pop world was not for him. So did being in a boy band work the same wonders for Matthew's love life as 'Acafellas' did for Will Schuester? 'God, it was so embarrassing!' he says now. *Elle* magazine sums up his feelings perfectly: the band's name may be 'pronounced "element" by the initiated, but [it is] referred to as "lament" by Morrison himself.'

Part of the problem was the lack of control Matthew

felt over his career: 'while I was rolling around with my entourage in my boy band, I had my people take care of everything.' Possibly the only thing he disliked more was a short stint on the popular soap, *As The World Turns*. 'I hated every second of being in a soap opera,' he told *Time Out New York*. 'I don't even put it on my résumé. It's a point of my life I like to forget. I have more respect for soap actors, though – it's literally like learning an entire script a night. So I had no life. I was someone's long-lost son, and when I left the show, they just replaced me with another actor.'

He returned to Broadway – and in style. A new show was opening at the Neil Simon Theatre on 15 August 2002 and Matthew was to be part of the originating cast. It almost didn't happen: another leading actor, James Carpinello, was originally scheduled to fill the role, but luck was on Matthew's side and he got to work on one of the Noughties' biggest hit musicals: *Hairspray*.

His role was the teen heartthrob, Link Larkin. Link is the dreamiest boy on *The Corny Collins Show*, a local celebrity among the Baltimore teens for his smooth dance moves and slicked-back hair. He plays the love interest for the feisty and 'pleasantly plump' main character, Tracy Turnblad. In the 2007 movie version, Zac Efron (from *High School Musical* fame) would fill Matthew's sexy dancing shoes.

Matthew may not have won the movie role for his breakout character, but he did start to garner more attention from Hollywood. He made his debut into the world of television and film with a series of small roles in *Sex and the City, Hack* and *Encino Man,* among others. His favourite TV part was in *Once Upon a Mattress* (2005), a television musical starring Carol Burnett.

But the stage was still where Matthew was to find the most success – until *Glee,* of course. He received a Tony nomination for Best Featured Actor in a Musical for his role in *The Light in the Piazza.* Set in the 1950s, it tells the story of a young American girl, Clare Johnson, who falls in love with a young Italian, Fabrizio Naccarelli (played by Matthew), while holidaying in Italy. There is a dark secret at the heart of the show, however, when it is revealed to the audience that Clare has suffered an accident as a child that has halted her mental development. The show was a hit on Broadway, although Matthew eventually left in late 2005.

Reviewers raved about his talent. While he was starring as Lt Joe Cable in the Lincoln Center's revival of Rodger's & Hammerstein's *South Pacific,* Eddie Varley of *Broadway World* wrote: 'Whether playing a sexually dysfunctional son in the comic *A Naked Girl on the Appian Way,* the troubled and yearning Duane in *10 Million Miles* or his Tony-nominated turn as Fabrizio in *The Light in the Piazza,* he's found a continual flow of substantial characters to embrace and bring to critically acclaimed life.'

During the interview with Varley held in May 2008,

Matthew also hinted about exciting news: 'Oh, man, I wish I could tell you Eddie, but I can't […] I want to tell you, but, it's just, it's all coming together, I'm working with people, you know them, I'm collaborating with this amazing team. I was inspired by the people who do it all, like Hugh Jackman, he's just an unbelievable performer, he gives everything he has to his performing. All the recent shows I've done I haven't been able to dance, so I feel that for my next move, I've got to dance again! […] I think it's going to blow people away.'

Could Matthew have been talking about *Glee*? He was cast during his time in *South Pacific*, so it certainly seems likely.

There were other rumours swirling around Matthew that he was aiming to make a move away from performing and move towards writing and producing, but *Glee* was to be the next big news for Morrison fans. His later words seemed to echo his former excitement: 'If I could have created a TV show for myself, this would have been it. So this is a dream job for me. It's great to see the crossover of Broadway on television.'

He might have been excited to see a mix of Broadway and TV, but the reality was extremely challenging. In an interview with *FOX All Access*, Matthew revealed: 'TV is different because it's 16-hour days on TV. If we're not filming, we're rushed to dance rehearsals or recording studios... it's like theatre boot camp.'

In fact, his audition for the role was relatively low-key for an actor with so much Broadway experience. As he explained, he 'didn't try to belt out a big showstopper. I came in and sang "Over the Rainbow" accompanying myself on the ukulele. I guess it worked.'

At the peak of *Glee*-mania, he was to display his winning talents at a Comic-Con 2009 panel. It was after the première of the pilot but before the show officially aired and the entire cast was riding a tidal wave of interest. On the panel, Matthew broke out into a spontaneous rendition of his audition tune. His natural charm, along with a powerful singing voice, quickly won over the fans in the audience. He was modest, too: 'The reason I got the part was the boots I was wearing. [The casting director] liked my boots.'

'I'm in love with you!' said Cory Monteith – also on the panel and echoing the sentiments of every fan in the room.

The hype surrounding *Glee* both scared and excited Matthew. Never before had he experienced publicity on this level – and the show hadn't even started yet. He was blown away by the statistics: 'More people saw the pilot of this show than saw me in the entire ten years I was on Broadway. Just the amount of people it reaches, you can't compare it.'

Not only that, but Matthew – by now a 'seasoned' actor at the age of 33 – was used to his privacy: 'I'm hugely into my anonymity, but this is part of being something special, so bring it on.' He was well aware that being the star of a big show like *Glee* would mean opening a Pandora's box of paparazzi and intense media scrutiny. But at no point in his wildest dreams did he imagine the series would become so big. 'I thought the show might struggle to find the right audience,' he admitted. Obviously that didn't prove to be the case as *Glee* connected with young and old across the globe.

Playing Will Schuester does give Matthew a taste of what his life might have been like, had he not taken big risks: moving away to New York, dropping out of college, throwing his name in the hat for every role that came his way. 'I'd love to say that this is a huge acting stretch for me, [but] this is kind of me... I probably shouldn't say that because I'm discrediting myself as an actor, but I feel like if I hadn't gone to New York, [I] would have gone to Chico State in Northern California, and I probably would have done theatre, come back to Southern California and taught at a performing arts high school.'

He has a lot of good things to say about a show that can push as many boundaries as *Glee*. For one, his character is torn between two women: his wife and the high-school guidance counsellor. In a normal TV show, he would be vilified for his attraction to another woman, but *Glee* manages to blur the lines. Should Will stay with his high-school sweetheart (who might also be borderline psychopathic) or go for the big-hearted and well-intentioned Emma Pillsbury, who is also completely mysophobic (afraid of germs)? 'You sure know how to pick them in the show!' observes Chris Colfer, who plays Kurt.

Will's love interests, however, have become two of the most fascinating women on TV. Jayma Mays, who plays Emma, made her first television appearance in the *Friends* spin-off *Joey* and later had recurring roles in hit TV shows such as *Entourage, Heroes* and *Ugly Betty*. Her biggest role before *Glee* was in the poorly reviewed but unexpected box-office hit movie, *Paul Blart: Mall Cop* (2009). She auditioned for *Glee* by singing 'Touch-A Touch-A Touch Me' from *The Rocky Horror Picture Show*. It was a nerve-wracking experience for someone without any professional singing experience: 'that was like the scariest thing I've ever had to do. My face got all red and I thought I was going to vomit. That was definitely out of the norm for me,' she told *Starry Constellation* magazine.

For those fans out there who are disappointed that they haven't heard much of Jayma's voice, Ryan Murphy said: 'I'm so going to have to get her to do that on the show.' Jayma herself is dying to sing: 'I keep saying I want to sing a country song – get back to my roots a little. You never know with them. They're so brilliant and they make it work, so you never know. They might have me rap or yodel. Maybe at the same time!' she laughed to *E! Online*.

But while Jayma's biggest impact on the show hasn't come from her vocals, her dress sense has inspired a whole host of Emma-wannabes. 'I like to call Emma's wardrobe quirky-chic!' the actress told *InStyle* magazine. 'While her outfits are always very put-together, they are still fun and flirty, with bows and flowers and the colors of sorbet.' Her character has even inspired blogs dedicated to her style, such as 'What Would Emma Pillsbury Wear?' and 'Emma Pillsbury's Box of Baubles'. The woman behind Jayma's amazing wardrobe is Lou Eyrich, who works as the costume designer on the show. 'Emma is the most fun [to dress], but that's only because I personally love that style of clothing', said Lou to *Entertainment Weekly*. To find Emma's wardrobe, she shops 'mostly J. Crew and Anthropologie. We also shop at Saks, especially the brand Milly. They do that great little tribute to the '60s. We started collecting the sweater chains all over town, especially antique stores and vintage clothing stores for the pins. I'm obsessed with sweater pins!'

Jessalyn Gilsig's character, Will's wife Terri, is the big villain of the show but Jessalyn sees the human side to her: 'I see Terri Schuester as pro-marriage. There is nothing she won't (and doesn't) do to save her marriage. Nothing. Some may be shocked by her choices, but I would ask those people, "Have you ever walked in the neighbourhood of a person you had a crush on even though it's on the other side of town for you, just in hopes of running into them? Have you ever pretended to have seen a movie they loved? Or laughed at a joke they told that you weren't sure was funny?" If so, don't judge Terri. As her sister Kendra explains, deceit may be the basis of a healthy marriage.'

Jessalyn also loves to joke around with Jayma and Matthew about their characters' love triangle. She told *Inside the Box*: 'I would give them so much grief, like basically Emma is a home wrecker. You know, just because she has a bob and she has red hair and she wears brooches, she's so sweet and so amazing? No, obviously she's a home wrecker. Step off my man, girl. I'm gonna get you! We had a lot of fun; we had so much fun with that.'

It seems Jessalyn has a Midas touch when it comes to the shows she has worked on. She starred simultaneously in two hit shows: Ryan Murphy's *Nip/Tuck* and the acclaimed drama *Prison Break*, while also fitting in recurring roles on *Heroes* and *CSI: NY*. It was her turn as the sexaholic Gina Russo on *Nip/Tuck* that ensured she was invited back to join Murphy on his next project, *Glee*, and he penned the part of Terri with the actress in mind. 'They'd already cast Matt, and Ryan wanted me to meet him, you know to just come in and see how we looked as a couple,' Jessalyn told *TV.com*. 'Obviously I was thrilled. My time on *Nip/Tuck* was one of the best experiences I've had since starting as an actor.'

Terri is another character who doesn't get to sing, but that doesn't mean Jessalyn wouldn't like to try. In fact, she thinks that Terri should sing the Pussycat Dolls' classic 'Don't Cha' now that Will has left her for Emma. 'The most challenging part of the role so far has been to restrain myself from singing or dancing when I'm hanging around set in hopes that someone will give me a song to sing,' said Jessalyn. 'I am surrounded every day by Tony-nominated Broadway stars, so it's important that I sit on my hands and speak when spoken to. That way I hope to do the least amount of damage possible.'

There's a good chance she might get to sing, especially as Ryan Murphy likes to push the cast's skills as far as possible. Matthew Morrison loves the fact that he gets to use all his musical talents, including those he'd buried deep in his past, but he could never have predicted that time spent with a break-dancing crew in the eighth grade listening to rap music and imitating Dr. Dre would lead to him rapping Kanye West in front of millions of TV viewers. Offered the choice of any song to perform on *Glee*, his answer is simple: 'Viva La Vida' by Coldplay, with the immense build-up of strings and orchestra behind him.

Inspired by bands such as Coldplay, along with a rapidly growing fan base to boost his confidence, Matthew looks set to break into the popular music scene once again, although this time on his own terms. In early 2010, he signed to Mercury Records. He wants to reinvent the American Bandstand, big band style of music. 'I would consider it a classier Justin Timberlake album,' he said of his work. 'It's going to be me and a big orchestra, but also with beats.'

In an interview with *Parade* magazine, he revealed: 'It's sort of in the style of Michael Bublé, or maybe you could call it Dean Martin-esque. It's just me and a big orchestra doing some standards and original songs. No rapping, unfortunately. Hopefully, I'm going to be working with David Foster to write some stuff.'

One thing he doesn't want to undertake, however, is the *Glee* tour around the United States. 'I don't think I'm going to be involved in that,' he told JustJared.com. 'Mr. Schuester likes to take his summer break.'

As long as Matthew doesn't take a break from *Glee*, the fans will be more than happy.

CHAPTER EIGHT

THE GOLD STAR

Lea Michele's *Glee* career began with a lucky accident – quite literally. Right before her audition at the FOX studio lot in Los Angeles, she got into a major car accident and totalled her car, then abandoned the still-smoking vehicle on Pico Boulevard. She walked in to sing for Ryan Murphy while still removing pieces of glass from her hair. 'There was construction and confusion,' she explained to *New York* magazine. 'I hear you have to crash your car once in California before you can be initiated as a true L.A. resident. So for me, I don't consider it a problem. I consider it, "Okay, good! Got that out of the way. Now I live here."'

It's a story that could have been written straight into the storyline of her exceedingly ambitious character,

Rachel 'Barbra' Berry. There's no way that Rachel would have let a small thing like crashing a car prevent her from getting to an audition. As Lea admits, 'It was such a Rachel Berry thing to do.' Showing such determination to get the part – and still having the chops to belt out a wicked rendition of 'On My Own' from *Les Misérables* despite the shock of the accident – was all the producers needed to see and they offered her the role on the spot.

But the crash might have been avoided, had Ryan Murphy been clear to Lea just how much they wanted her to play Rachel. She herself remembers feeling incredibly nervous (which probably didn't help her driving much), when actually Ryan had written the role of Rachel with Lea in mind: 'I wish he'd told me that before my audition because I would have definitely been a lot less nervous but it's good that I didn't know, because I really fought for it.'

So how did this young actress, only 22 at the time of her audition, get to have a major TV role written especially for her? She has had an extraordinary career in the build-up to *Glee*, and it all started with a chance audition when she was just 8 years old.

Lea Michele was born Lea Michele Sarfati on 29 August 1986 in New York's The Bronx. Her mother, Edith, was an Italian-American Catholic nurse and her father, Marc, was a deli owner with Spanish-Sephardic Jewish ancestry.

She first caught the musical theatre bug at 8 years old when her best friend, Chloe, took her to see a variety of musicals: 'We went to see *Camelot* and I think that I fell asleep, and then we went to see *Cats* and I was scared. Finally, we went to go see *The Phantom of the Opera*, and I think that was the first time that I really saw the beauty of theatre and I instantly fell in love with it.'

This was also the age that Lea was at her most precocious. In fact, she thinks she was most like Rachel then: 'I draw a lot of inspiration from myself when I was very young. I was very much like Rachel when I was, like, 8 or 9. I always wanted to perform. Every Christmas video is me standing in front of my family singing "Santa Baby" and putting on a mini-concert for my whole family.'

The chance for Lea to show off her talent came with an open call for young Cosette in *Les Misérables*. Again, it was Lea's friend who was desperate to go and audition, but Chloe's father suffered a heart attack the night before and her mother was therefore unable to drive her to the auditions: 'Her mother asked if we would take her since it was such a huge dream of hers, and for whatever reason I decided that I wanted to audition as well. I had been listening to the soundtrack of *Phantom* nonstop and had memorised "Angel of Music". I went in and sang at the open call "Angel of Music" a cappella and I ended up booking it right then and there, and that's what started it all for me.'

For Lea, this was the beginning of something special and awoke an underlying talent that she didn't know she had. 'I haven't stopped singing since,' she admits.

Something about the outgoing little girl caught the casting director's eye and her talent was confirmed when director Richard Jay-Alexander agreed to book her straightaway. Lea isn't the first actress to get her start as Young Cosette in the Broadway production of *Les Misérables* either. Many young stars such as Lacey Chabert from *Mean Girls* and *Desperate Housewives'* Andrea Bowen started out as the mistreated young girl who grows up to fall in love with Jean Valjean.

The Sarfati family were unbelievably proud and excited for their little girl and so they moved closer to New York – to Tenafly, New Jersey – to make the commute between home and the stage a great deal easier. Lea's mum also quit her job as a nurse to support her daughter full time.

Unlike many parents who try to live vicariously through their children by pushing them into show business, Lea's parents were very relaxed and willing to let their child's career unfold naturally. She credits them with helping her land those early roles, not by pushing her to be the best, but by being so laid back.

The actress told *Broadway Buzz*: 'The one thing you will hear from anyone who ever worked with me – and I truly believe it's what helped me get so many jobs as a young kid – is that I have the coolest, most easygoing parents. Let me tell you, there were some crazy, crazy, crazy mothers out there. My parents would say, "This [audition] is not a big deal," whereas other parents would look at their children and say, "You need to get this job."'

Being an only child helped too – her parents were able to devote all their energy to helping her succeed: 'My parents just helped keep it real for me, and the casts that I worked with and the stage managements just appreciated that.'

They must have been doing something right because immediately after her turn as young Cosette, Lea landed her next part as 'The Little Girl' with the originating cast of *Ragtime* in Toronto, Ontario, Canada (the show later moved to Broadway, where she opened in the same role). Opening on 8 December 1996, *Ragtime* was an epic portrait of early twentieth-century America, intertwining the lives of three families: a wealthy New Rochelle clan, a Harlem ragtime pianist, and a Latvian immigrant and his young daughter. It went on to receive 12 Tony Award nominations in 1998, including the Tony Award for Best Musical.

Together, Lea and her mum moved to Canada, leaving her dad behind to run his deli store. '[My mom] left my dad at home with our dog and our two cats for an entire year. My parents met when they were about 14 years old and they had never been apart. But my mom, having known nothing about this business, knew who Audra McDonald was and knew who Brian Stokes Mitchell was, and she realized that [*Ragtime*] was the best education I could ever get. Going to Canada and working with Peter Friedman, Marin Mazzie, Brian Stokes Mitchell and Audra McDonald was a masterclass,' she told *Broadway World*.

Indeed, *Ragtime* led her to audition for her most famous role before *Glee* – that of Wendla Bergmann in *Spring Awakening,* a modern adaptation of the controversial play by Frank Wedekind (1891). Touching on a whole range of adolescent issues from masturbation and sexual exploration to rape, pregnancy and abortion, it was originally banned in its native Germany. The modern version retains the same setting – late nineteenth-century Germany – but tells the story through alternative rock music written by Duncan Sheikh.

Lea was only 14 at the time but she absolutely fell in love with the complicated role of the young girl whose lack of sexual education leads her to becoming pregnant and eventually dying from a botched abortion. The opportunity came at the perfect time for her – *Spring Awakening* was in the 'workshop' stage, which meant that the directors and cast were still reading through the script and ironing out all the kinks before the show transferred to Broadway. This meant that she didn't have to commit to performing full-time, not just yet. Lea took full advantage of the break and decided to fit in a few years of 'normal' high school life before returning to New York.

She looks back on her time at Tenafly High School, New Jersey, fondly, although she also admits that 'all it did was reconfirm that I wanted to be an actor and get out of high school as quickly as I could.' Lea wasn't very popular in school, instead preferring to focus on singing and getting good grades. 'I wasn't a partier, I wasn't a wild kid,' she told *Edge* magazine. 'I was the one going to work every night and practicing at home, singing. But that's who I was. It may not have been accepted but I was proud to be me and trust that.' She played volleyball and joined the debate team but tended to shy away from acting. Only once did she perform in a school play, but in general, she 'wanted to give other kids the opportunity to act who didn't otherwise get to perform.' Interestingly, her least favourite memories are of her school choir – and *Glee* brings it all back with a vengeance: 'Every time we're in the choir room, I get these awful pangs and memories. It was terrible.'

By her senior year she had booked yet another Broadway show – *Fiddler on the Roof*: 'I booked *Fiddler on the Roof* and that was my third Broadway show and it was pretty unbelievable because there was like, a three-year gap between *Ragtime* and *Fiddler*, and it reminded me that there was still something there and I shouldn't give up – that I could not work for three years and it was still there for me.'

She still made time to go to prom, though. 'It was so lame,' she told *TV Guide*. 'So lame! I enjoyed the normal teenager experiences, but every time I went to them it confirmed to me that I was really happy with the decisions I was making in my life. We had this rooftop prom at this gorgeous place and nobody was on the dance floor! They were all on the roof smoking cigarettes and the boys were smoking cigars, trying to be all cool.'

Now it was decision time for Lea. She had won a place at the prestigious Tisch School of the Arts at NYU (the same college Matthew Morrison had dropped out of a few years earlier), but her acceptance would mean giving up on auditions and performing for a while. So instead, she put college on hold, packed up her bags and moved to the Big City on her own to continue living the dream.

Postponing college turned out to be the easy part. Lea had to deal with an even more difficult choice when she was offered her dream role as Éponine in *Les Misérables* at the same time as *Spring Awakening* was due to open on Broadway. Despite longing to play Éponine, she had devoted six long years of workshops and off-Broadway performances to perfecting the character of Wendla and ultimately, she chose to stay with *Spring Awakening*.

The show opened to enormous critical acclaim and

Lea herself was nominated for a Drama Desk Award in the category of Outstanding Actress in a Musical for her performance. *Spring Awakening* also received 11 Tony Award nominations in 2007, winning eight, including Tonys for Best Musical, Direction, Book, Score and Featured Actor.

Theatre Mania had nothing but good things to say about the main characters in its review of the opening night in December 2006: 'The brooding, handsome Groff seizes his moments with gusto; Gallagher is nothing short of galvanic; and the gorgeous-voiced Michele is absolutely heartbreaking.' The *New York Times* was similarly effusive in its praise: 'The singing throughout is impassioned and affecting, giving powerful voice to the blend of melancholy and hope in the songs.'

In a way, the show was the perfect training for *Glee*. The music of *Spring Awakening* is highly contemporary and a hugely different change of pace to big Broadway musicals such as *Les Misérables*. 'I was raised on the classic Broadway shows, but there's another side of me that's listening to Kelly Clarkson and rockin' out to pop music,' she writes on her official Myspace (leamichelemusic). 'That's the amazing thing about [*Spring Awakening*] – the way that I grew up listening to Alanis Morissette's "Ironic" or the way that girls blast "Since U Been Gone" is the same way you can blast "Bitch of Living" or "Don't Do Sadness."'

The most talked-about moment of *Spring Awakening* is the infamous sex scene between Lea's character Wendla and Melchior, who was played at the time by her best friend, Jonathan Groff. Wendla ends up topless on stage as the two explore their sexuality for the first time. 'I just thought I was alone with Jonathan,' she told *Allure* magazine. 'The scene wasn't that raunchy when I was 14. It was made more age-appropriate as I got older.' She was careful when her family was in the audience, though. 'They knew when to cover their eyes. When my dad would come, I would not expose myself that night. For. Sure.' Her parents weren't unhappy with the scene – quite the opposite, as they respected Lea and the director enough to know that they would never make compromising decisions.

Lea's enormous success in the part made her one of the most recognisable cast members when the pilot for *Glee* aired for the very first time on US television. At Comic-Con 2009, it became a running joke as audience member after audience member gushed over how amazing Lea was in *Spring Awakening* – practically ignoring all the other actors on the panel. Her Broadway success and obvious talent gave *Glee* credibility in the music world, especially as it was giving gifted young people the chance to showcase their abilities when they would otherwise be less accessible to mainstream audiences. One (obviously very short-sighted) casting director dubbed Lea 'too ethnic-looking and not pretty enough for television'. *Glee* took a chance where perhaps others weren't willing to do so.

It was her standout performance in *Spring Awakening* that led her to the role of Rachel Berry, even though she didn't know it at the time. In fact, it was Lea's best friend Jonathan Groff who pointed Ryan Murphy in her direction. At the time, Groff had taken a month off the show to fly out to LA and shoot a pilot for Murphy's new concept TV show *Pretty/Handsome* (2008).

By happy coincidence Lea was at a loose end at the same time. In late 2007, the Broadway stagehands went on strike, temporarily shutting down the Eugene O'Neill Theater where *Spring Awakening* was being performed. She suggested to Jonathan: 'Instead of sitting on my hands in New York, why don't I come visit you in California?' During her visit, Jonathan took her out to dinner with Murphy and Lea was instantly impressed by the charismatic writer with big ideas, describing him as 'one of the most loyal, caring, smart people you will ever meet.' But she had no idea that she had also made a great impression on Murphy, so much so that when he began work on the script for *Glee*, he already knew who would play his Glee Club star.

Spurred on by Jonathan's success, when the time came for Lea to leave *Spring Awakening*, she made the move to Los Angeles. She had decided that finally, it was the right time for her to play her dream musical theatre role and she was cast as Éponine in *Les Misérables* at LA's Hollywood Bowl. At the same time, she wanted to see if she could get work on a television show. One of her goals was to be cast as a victim on the popular hospital drama, *Grey's Anatomy*. She was up for reading any parts that came her way, but knew she wouldn't settle for just any role: 'I'd been getting so many scripts that were the same character over and over again: the beautiful, gorgeous wealthy girl.'

Glee was her second audition. Already she was thrilled at the prospect of playing the bubbly, but self-centred star of the Glee Club. 'I hadn't read a script or a character as funny, as outgoing, and as different as Rachel.'

Murphy may have already decided that Lea was his girl, but he had to convince the producers and so she still had to audition. Except Murphy was so sure Lea was the one, he didn't invite anyone else to the call-backs. But it didn't matter: ultimately, Lea floored everyone with her flawless rendition of 'On My Own' – despite the car accident, as we have seen before. But the role of Rachel Berry is more than just a voice and Lea had to prove she had the acting chops too. However, the character came easily to her and she managed to slip some perfect 'Rachel Berry' moments into her audition – when the pianist playing her audition song skipped the second verse, she snapped around and told him that she had to sing the entire song. When the producers started to giggle during one of her monologues, she announced: 'This is supposed to be my serious part. Stop laughing! I want to see you crying this time.' They loved it, they loved *her* and everyone agreed she was Rachel, through and through.

After she got the part, Lea asked Murphy: 'Do you remember me?' That's when he revealed that he had written the character with her in mind. For the budding actress, there couldn't be a higher compliment.

There was also a lot of pressure on young Lea. A big part of the show's success rested on whether she could make Rachel both arrogant *and* accessible to viewers – she had to be proud of her talent and yet endearing enough to be liked. She is a complex character on a voyage of self-discovery through high school. What kind of background would create a creature like Rachel, so self-assured yet so vulnerable? Lea talked about Rachel's probable childhood to *TV Guide*: 'Well, Rachel was raised by two gay men in Ohio, and I think that she grew up watching a lot of classic movies – *Funny Girl* and *Cabaret*, *West Side Story* – I definitely think that she was very much like me as a child, talking at a very young age and always putting on shows in her living room. Her fathers have taught her to be proud of who she is and comfortable in her own skin.'

Rachel also grows a lot through the first thirteen episodes. The show follows her as she struggles to gain acceptance within the group and finds her first proper friendships: '[One thing] I have learned is just how much this is Rachel's journey to becoming a team player and learning who she is within this group. You look at Rachel and realize that she is not someone who needs help speaking her mind.'

We also watch as Rachel struggles through the trials and pitfalls of first love. Her love is for Finn Hudson, the handsome quarterback, but she also experiences a heady schoolgirl crush on her choir teacher, Mr. Schuester, and a brief fling with Glee Club's resident bad boy, Puck. Ryan Murphy was surprised by the audience's reaction to the Rachel-Puck episode: they loved it. He expected people to 'ship' (the internet fan term for 'root for' or 'support') Finn and Rachel to get together but instead there was a growing support for Rachel and Puck. 'I thought that was very strange and bizarre. I had no idea – I thought that people would not like them together. I thought people would root for her to be with Finn,' said Murphy.

And what of Lea's own love life? Playing the gorgeous female lead in a hit show means that she appears constantly on the covers of celebrity magazines, all trying to figure out exactly what is going on behind closed doors. Particularly vehement were the rumours she and Cory Monteith (who plays Finn) were a couple. Then it was Lea and Mark Salling (Puck). 'Every week I'm rumoured to be dating a different *Glee* cast member and it is hysterical. But none of us are dating each other. I will say that much.'

In fact, being so successful has made it harder for Lea to find someone. It's not surprising if guys are intimidated by the beautiful actress who appears to have it all – brains, beauty, a great singing voice – all that and a fun, bubbly personality to boot: 'Contrary to belief, guys are not blowing up my phone trying to date me at the moment. I am very happy, I'll say that, but I will never tell if I am dating someone.'

But dealing with rumours and figuring out the character of Rachel were not the only challenge for Lea. She is a trained Broadway actress, but she had never had any experience of TV before and now, all of a sudden she was working in television full time.

Many actors who make the transition from theatre to the small (or big) screen have trouble toning down their 'stage voice' or controlling their actions to make them appear more natural on camera. In theatre the most important thing is to be seen and heard correctly, whereas on camera, actions need to be more subtle in order to avoid seeming insincere. Yet because Rachel is an over-the-top character, Lea's theatrical training was extremely useful in portraying her energy: 'I was kind of just thrown into this,' she told the *Washington Post*. 'This is one of the first television jobs I've ever had. The character I'm playing is really outgoing – she performs in her everyday life as though she's performing in front of a huge audience.' Undoubtedly it also helps that Lea gets to sing every episode. Singing is her comfort zone, her forte, and where she really helps Rachel Berry to shine.

GLEEFUL! MOMENT

Lea loves body art and has several tattoos, including the 'Imagine' tattoo on one foot, a butterfly inspired by the set of Spring Awakening on her other foot, a Rachel Berry-esque gold star on her wrist, two musical notes that represent the notes 'Ma ma' from 'Bohemian Rhapsody' by Queen on her shoulder and 'I Believe' is written on the inside of her right wrist.

And she must be doing something right, because in late 2009, Lea was nominated for a Teen Choice Award for Choice TV Breakout Star. That was swiftly followed by a win at the 2009 Satellite Award for Best Actress in a Series, beating several seasoned television performers such as Edie Falco (*Nurse Jackie*), Toni Collette (*United States of Tara*) and Tina Fey (*30 Rock*).

In early 2010, Lea had another nomination, this time for a prestigious Golden Globe Award for Best Actress in a TV Series (Musical or Comedy). She told *Entertainment Weekly* about the moment when she heard her nomination: 'So I decided to turn the TV on, and the minute I turned the TV on, the first name I heard was my name. It was crazy. I just couldn't believe – and I still can't believe – that I was nominated in the category that I'm in, with the calibre of actresses I'm amongst. It's such an out-of-body experience, really.' Once again she was up against Edie Falco and Tina Fey as well as Courtney Cox (*Cougar Town*). The eventual winner was Toni Colette.

Even though she didn't win this time, just the nomination was something to be immensely proud of. Lea's mum could barely get over her excitement: 'I will give you a proper congratulations when I snap out of this shock,' she told her daughter. And she wasn't just congratulating Lea for the nomination for Best Actress – there were also nominations for Best Television Series (Musical or Comedy), Best Actor in a (Musical or Comedy) for Matthew Morrison and Jane Lynch was up for Best Supporting Actress in a (Musical or Comedy). For *Glee*, this was a big night all around. But did the producers let them celebrate? Not a chance because they had the next nine episodes to film to catch up with all the hype!

This being her first nomination, Lea wasn't fussed about winning or losing. 'I'm just really excited to get to go,' she told *Entertainment Weekly*. 'I'm gonna bring my mom. I just want to sit back and be a fly on the wall, that's really all I want to do. I just want to sit, watch everyone, see all the people who are there, and probably have a heart attack when they announce the nominees for my category. To hear my name between Edie Falco and Toni Colette is just crazy.'

Luckily she has the work to keep her grounded: the announcement that *Glee* was signed for a second season meant new storylines, new guest stars and most importantly, new songs. For Lea, it also brought the exciting news that her best friend and *Spring Awakening* co-star, Jonathan Groff, was to join her on the show.

So what's on the horizon for Lea? Like Matthew Morrison, she has been signed up to Columbia Records with the opportunity to record her own solo album. With her voice already dominating on the *Glee* albums, there's no doubt that a solo project would be a success. Her only problem now is to decide which direction to take, as it seems all options are open to her. 'Lea has tried different songs and already thought, "Maybe I like doing rock,"' revealed Ryan Murphy. 'Her album is not going to be Broadway stuff – she'll sit with producers and come up with her own concept.'

She's also got the big screen in her sights as well, as she sets out to conquer the movie world – admittedly the animated kind for now. In 2011, Lea is to star alongside Kristin Chenoweth as the voice of Dorothy in the animated *Dorothy of Oz*. One thing's for sure: her star will only get brighter as time goes on. Better start stocking up on those shiny gold-star stickers!

CHAPTER NINE
DUMB JOCKS

Cory Monteith and Mark Salling are both 27 – ten years older than the high-school seniors they play in *Glee*. But they're by no means the first actors to play kids much younger than themselves. Rachel McAdams was 24 when she portrayed the fantastically evil Regina George in *Mean Girls* (2004). And they're both still younger than Trevor Donovan in *90210*, who is 31 and playing an 18-year-old.

'I love it,' said Cory. 'I never really got to experience high school so [the show] is like giving me a second chance.'

Cory has never hidden the fact that he dropped out of high school after only one year. 'I flipped off high school at a very young age,' he shrugs, talking to the *Toronto Star*. 'I had bigger fish to fry, getting in trouble with all my friends and running away from home and bulls—t like that.'

In fact, he would never have enjoyed the full on American high-school experience, had he stayed on in school, for one simple reason – he's Canadian. Born in Calgary, Alberta, his family moved to Victoria, British Columbia when Cory was just a small boy. After dropping out of school, he worked a lot of odd jobs. His first was on a car lot when he was only 13. After that, he worked in Walmart as a people greeter, driving a school bus, as a roofer and a cab driver.

His biggest love was music and Cory classifies himself as a drummer. You can see his skills in the pilot episode when he takes over the drums during 'Don't Stop Believing". When he was 17, he played in a progressive new metal band in Victoria called New Westminster. 'It wasn't anything terribly compelling,' he told *Toronto Star*. 'Kind of King Crimson meets Queens of the Stone Age. Interesting stuff. It sure wasn't *Glee*.' In fact, the band even had some interest from Atlantic Records, who sent up their A&R team to check them out. It wasn't meant to be, although he remembers being incredibly excited at the time, but back then, something about his life just wasn't fulfilling: 'I was getting by, for sure. I was making a good living. But it really wasn't a life, per se.'

Destiny had other plans for Cory. While working as a cab driver, someone told him, 'You know Cory, you should be an actor'. To such a free spirit, the idea of being able to act for a living must have had its appeal, but it was an impossible dream for someone living miles from any casting opportunities. So when Cory was 20 years old, he boarded the ferry to Vancouver Island and settled in the big city itself, Vancouver, B.C.

Vancouver is known as Hollywood North and a lot of big-budget American films and TV shows are shot there to save money. One major example is the *Twilight* franchise. While the original *Twilight* movie was filmed in Portland, Oregon, director Chris Weitz chose to move proceedings up to Vancouver for *New Moon*.

Of course, acting success doesn't often happen overnight and budding Canadian actors and actresses flock to Vancouver in the same way that Americans like Matthew Morrison might leave for New York or Los Angeles. Cory picked up a job as a waiter to earn some extra cash while he waited for his big break. 'The description of success as an actor in Canada is not having to work another job,' he remarks dryly. 'That goes for 98% of actors – myself included for the majority of my career.'

He confesses that he wasn't very good at serving tables. 'I worked at an all-cake restaurant [called True Confections],' he told Conan O'Brien on *The Tonight Show*. But he'd always be in the back room reading scripts rather than concentrating on delivering good customer service. 'I always forgot to give them a fork,' he revealed.

He did start to have some acting success, however, and landed bit parts in *Smallville* and *Supernatural*, along with films such as *Whisper* and *Deck the Halls*. But his biggest break before *Glee* came when he won a role in the TV drama, *Kyle XY*. It's a show about a boy who wakes up in a forest with amnesia: his quest is to find out who he is and why he has no memories. On the posters, Kyle is shown as having no belly button. Cory's recurring role as Charlie Tanner proved enough for him to attract the interest of an American agent, who agreed to represent him and put him forward for shows like *Glee*. He was 24 years old at the time.

Before *Glee* arrived on the scene, he auditioned for anything under the sun. Not everything went well. Cory's worst audition was for the movie *Sky High for Disney*, a film about a floating high school for the children of superheroes. Cory simply could not overcome his nervousness. 'I went in and I was so nervous that I forgot all my lines,' he told cast mates Matthew Morrison and Chris Colfer on AOL's *Outside the Box*. 'The casting director said I could just read the lines so I took them out and they were upside down. I then fumbled them around and then dropped them on the floor. I was so nervous.'

In retrospect, it's no doubt that all the bad auditions

were just experience leading up to his biggest break yet. Actors often say that the hardest thing to deal with is rejection, but the most important thing is to get back up and keep trying again and again. You never know when that big break is just around the corner – even if it's for something you don't expect, or something that you believe you have no chance of getting.

Cory wasn't sure of his chances when his manager told him about *Glee*. His age wasn't such a problem – as we have seen, older actors often take on the role of teenagers – but this was a musical television show. Surely they would be looking for someone with extensive singing and dancing experience? 'I had no background in musical theatre. Not even a month ago Lea Michele [Rachel on *Glee*] took me to *Rock of Ages* – it was the first Broadway musical I'd seen,' Monteith told the *National Post*.

But what did he have to lose? After some encouragement from his manager, he sent in a tape of the only musical skills he had: his drumming. 'I was drumming on the back of some Tupperware boxes with unsharpened pencils,' he said. Hardly the professional audition tape that the *Glee* producers might have been expecting, but it showed enough of his obvious talent that they were intrigued. They asked for more – and this time, with singing.

He described the second audition process to Backstage.com: 'I sent an audition tape from Canada.

That was the first time I'd ever auditioned and sung; I'd never done anything like that before. I'd never sent a tape of myself singing; I'd never sung for anybody.' The tape was of Cory singing REO Speedwagon's 'Can't Fight This Feeling' – 'but I did it like an 80s music video where I'm all looking out into the distance. It was really cheesy.'

Again, producers were intrigued. But Finn was proving to be one of the most difficult roles to cast for. So they asked Cory to meet with them in person – but he would have to make his own way from Vancouver to LA. So, the actor got in his car and drove the five-and-a-half hours to the City of Angels.

Unfortunately, just getting there wasn't enough. There were still a lot of talented actors in the running for Finn – the last role to be cast. 'When I got into the call-back, there were, like, 25 or 30 other dudes, all up for the same part. We all looked the same: 30 tall, quarterback-looking dudes, all in one room,' he told the *Toronto Star*. 'My agent hooked me up with [*Glee* musical director Brad Ellis], cause he was the guy who was going to be the piano accompaniment for the auditions. So I spent a couple hours with him on the weekend before the test, and I said, "This is the song I want to sing. Can you teach me how to sing it?" I had no idea what I was doing. I thought they wanted musical theatre, so I was going to sing a song from *Rent*. We chose different songs after working together – it ended up being Billy Joel.'

DUMB JOCKS

Robert J. Ulrich, of Ulrich/Dawson/Kritzer Casting, was overseeing the casting process and he described the difficulty they had in finding the perfect Finn: 'It was important that Finn be a very good singer, but he also had to be a guy's guy, a strapping football star, or the character wouldn't work. He also had to play a naïve, not stupid, quality. It was a difficult character – one that we went to network with many times before we found Cory [Monteith].'

He might have been up against some stiff competition, but Cory came out on top. The producers saw that he could convincingly play both the popular jock and the sensitive singer. Those competing sides of Finn's personality form the basis of his character. 'He's serving two masters: trying to be the popular guy with the cheerleader girlfriend and trying to follow his dreams and be with the girl he actually likes,' Cory explained to *Entertainment Weekly*.

The girl he likes, of course, is Rachel Berry – the overly ambitious young ingénue with the voice of an angel, played by Lea. It's by no means love at first sight for Finn, however, and Rachel complains she feels invisible to him. Cory tried to deconstruct their relationship to *Australian TV Week*. 'Finn is quite scared of Rachel when he first meets her,' he laughed. 'He doesn't understand her intensity or why she talks so much – he's put off. But there's something enchanting about her because she possess this skill and talent that he wants to find in himself. Their relationship develops quickly.'

One of the great highlights of the show and one of the reasons why it's so captivating is the chemistry between Finn and Rachel. Both characters have major flaws but when they're together, they bring out each other's best qualities. It's this chemistry that has driven *Glee* fans to speculate about a real-life relationship between Cory and Lea. Fans often find it hard to believe that two people can have so much chemistry on screen without it carrying on behind-the-scenes. Every moment the actors spent together off screen – and in the autumn of 2009, that seemed to be all the time – was scrutinised. When Lea took Cory to see his first musical, was that a date? 'He's great, and he makes me laugh,' Lea replied to *OK! Magazine* in early November 2009 when asked about Cory. In the same interview, Cory said, 'We've become very close friends.' Neither was seen as denying a relationship – in fact, this only further fuelled the rumours!

A month later and it was going too far for Cory and Lea. 'First of all, no, we're not dating,' he told the *National Post*. 'We're like oil and water, complete opposites. I couldn't imagine what our dating life would be like. Pretty intense.'

You can't blame the fans for trying, especially as it has happened successfully in the past. Penn Badgley and Blake Lively from *Gossip Girl* have managed to take their relationship from the cameras to real life. However, Cory thinks that mixing working relationship with dating is too much of a challenge: 'That seems really difficult,' he told American magazine *People*. 'That seems like it would be tricky.' And he went on to assure fans: 'I'm single.'

Of course, it doesn't help when fellow cast member Mark Salling (who plays football player Noah 'Puck' Puckerman) jokes around about on-set intrigue. 'It's all true. Every little word is true,' he said to *People* magazine of the relationship dramas. 'Every little thing you read in those magazines is true. Spot on.' Many fans won't take this in the tongue-in-cheek way that Mark meant it, but the actor simply wouldn't be able to play Puck without throwing out a few cheeky bad-boy vibes.

Born and raised in Dallas, Texas, Mark attended the Los Angeles Music Academy and then acted in films such as *Children of the Corn IV* (1996) and *The Graveyard* (2006). Although *Glee* is his first big acting gig, he has been in the music business for a while – singing, writing and playing guitar under his musical stage name, Jericho. He released his debut album *Smoke Screens* in 2008. Music has always been in his blood: 'I've been playing piano since I was five, and started writing when I was six or seven. It was never a revelation I had, it was just what I did. Playing music was always a part of my life, I don't know anything else,' he told About.com.

His path into *Glee* was the result of a struggling music career: 'I was playing music and struggling from paycheck to paycheck and not really seeing my music take off the way I wanted. A couple of my students kept telling me that I needed to get on L.A. Casting because they're always looking for people who can play instruments or sing. I did a little research and sent out 100 packets to about 50 managers and agents. Out of all those people, one called me and submitted me for *Glee* that day in her office. I was pretty lucky.'

The character of Puck really evolved from the first time he is introduced in the pilot. But Mark wasn't a lot like his character in high school: 'I was kind of more of a hippie in high school, to be honest. I wrestled, I didn't play football, but yeah, I try to make the character my own and try to implement, you know, aspects of my personality into him. So hopefully you will be seeing me in some degree.' He also doesn't see a problem in being so much older than high-school age as it fits in with the character: 'I remember in the breakdown for the show, when they were describing his character in the very beginning, it's like Puck: a man-child. They described him as a man-child, so I figured a couple crow's-feet might be alright.' One thing he definitely can't get used to is the Mohawk: 'I'm so over the Mohawk,' he told *People* magazine. 'I'm not gonna lie – I hate the Mohawk.' He might hate it, but it hasn't stopped the gorgeous Mark Salling from attracting the attention of a number of ladies himself. Recently, he has been linked to *The Hills* star Audrina Patridge.

At least Cory and Mark's personal love lives are nowhere near as tricky as their characters. Not only is Finn caught up in a Rachel-Quinn-Puck love quadrangle but he has to deal with admiration from another source: Chris Colfer's Kurt. This addition gives him one of the most complicated story arcs of all the *Glee* kids. 'It's delicate,' he told *Entertainment Weekly*. 'How much does Finn know about how Kurt feels for him? How much of it does he understand? We were all very careful to make sure that we handled that with intelligence and character.'

Complicated as it might be, Cory has relished the opportunity to play such a great role. He's been forced to stretch his acting chops like never before and he's had to pick up a lot of new skills along the way. At first, he seemed quite overwhelmed by the challenge when he first realised what was required of him. The vocal training, for example, was completely new: 'Oh my God! I had no idea what I was getting myself into at all. I thought, okay, I can sing. I thought, you can sing or you can't, so show up and sing. But I had no idea that you make strange noises to make your voice sound better.'

Then there was the dancing. He told *Digital Journal*: 'Yeah, it was really hard, especially in the beginning, because we were learning how to work with a choreographer and shoot the show and prerecord the music, to learn the dance choreography, too. So I mean, at the beginning of the show, we were taking weeks to do some of these dance numbers. And near the end of the season, we were taking days. So I mean, everything had just gotten compacted and condensed. It's a huge workload alongside eight days to shoot an episode. So it's pretty much every moment that we're not shooting the show, we're learning the dance routines or choreographing the dance routines or recording the songs. So it's a lot. It's great that it's all good stuff.'

The intense dance schedule was new to the whole cast, but with almost no performance background whatsoever, Cory felt the pressure even more. 'It's been challenging to perform with talented, seasoned Broadway performers,' he said in reply to a viewer question on AOL's *Out of the Box*. Indeed, the experience has brought – almost dragged – Cory's talent out into the spotlight. With *Glee*'s schedule, there's no time for nerves or hesitation: you just have to go for it.

For every Cory, with little-to-no professional dance experience, there's a Harry Shum Jr., an amazing dancer with a career spanning dance films such as *You Got Served* (2004) and *Stomp the Yard* (2007) to performing on tour with Beyoncé and Mariah Carey. Harry plays 'Other Asian' Mike Chang, another New Directions

Glee wins the 2009 Screen Actors Guild Award for Outstanding Performance by an Ensemble in a Comedy Series!

Above left: Looking drop-dead gorgeous, Matthew Morrison and Lea Michele show off their awards.

Above right: Jane Lynch is definitely proud of hers. © *Matt Baron/Rex Features*

Below: More of the cast with their awards. © *Getty Images*

The cast were also winners at the 67th Annual Golden Globe Awards, taking home the gong for Best Series (Musical or Comedy).

Above left: Lea Michele with Ryan Murphy, *Glee*'s co-creator and executive producer.

Above right: She's got the golden ticket. Lea shows off the card that announced their win.

Below: The cast crowd around the coveted Golden Globe award.

Above: Two of *Glee*'s co-creators Brad Falchuk and Ian Brennan stand alongside *Glee* executive producer Dante Di Loreto.

Left: Everyone wants a piece of Ryan Murphy – especially now *Glee* has become such a massive success! © *Getty Images*

Pre-Glee: Jane Lynch

Above: Check out Jane Lynch (*top, middle*) in *The Real Life Brady Bunch*
on 17 October 1990.

Below: Jane with Jennifer Coolidge in Christopher Guest's cult hit movie
Best in Show (2000).

Pre-Glee: Jane Lynch

Above: In 2005, Jane starred alongside Steve Carell in *The 40-Year-Old Virgin*.
© *Universal/Everett/ Rex Features*

Left: She also got the chance to film *Julie & Julia* with one of her idols, Meryl Streep. © *Getty Images*

Pre-Glee: Lea Michele, Amber Riley and Kevin McHale

Above left: Lea at the opening night of *Spring Awakening* on 15 June 2006.
© *Carolyn Contino/BEI/ Rex Features*

Above right: At 17, Amber tried and failed to make it on to *American Idol*; only a few years later she was a guest star at the *American Idol* Top 13 Party in Los Angeles.
© *Peter Brooker/ Rex Features*

Below: Kevin McHale with the other members of the boyband NLT (Not Like Them) on 8 April 2008.
© *Bryan Bedder/ Getty Images*

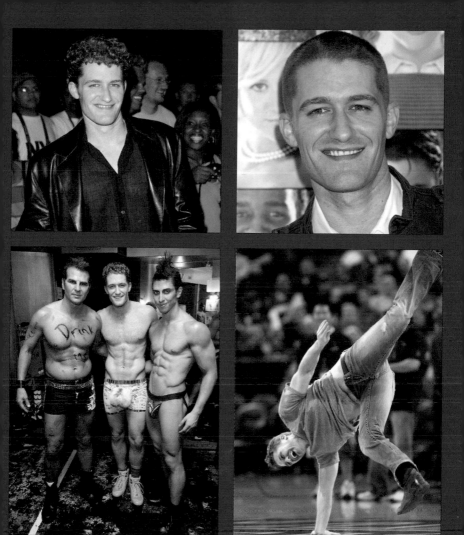

Pre-Glee: Matthew Morrison

Above: At the opening night of the musical *Hairspray* on Broadway on 15 August 2002 (*left*) and at the premiere of the film adaptation of *Hairspray* on 16 July 2007 (*right*). Matthew Morrison was the original Link Larkin on Broadway. © *M Baron and Erik C. Pendzich / Rex Features*

Below left: Stripped down for the Broadway Bares 18: Wonderland on 22 June 2008. © *Getty Images*

Below right: Showing off his well known dance moves at an NBA game in November 2009. © *PA Photos*

Glee mania begins!

Above: Cast and cheerleaders gather together to celebrate all things *Glee*!

© Getty Images

Below: Fans go crazy when the cast visit the Borders bookstore in New York.

© Charles Sykes/ Rex Features

football team convert. Pre-*Glee*, one of his most famous roles is as a dancing silhouette for the now infamous iPod commercials. Not one to rest on his laurels, in the break between filming the first thirteen episodes and the last nine, Harry has been choreographing, producing and performing in an online series called *LXD – League of Extraordinary Dancers*.

But *Glee* was his big break. 'It definitely has changed my life,' he told the *Philippines Inquirer*. Harry was born in Costa Rica and speaks Spanish, Chinese and English. His parents moved up to Los Angeles to give their three children (Harry has two older sisters) a better life. Like his character, Harry discovered dancing in high school because a few other cool kids joined: 'Early in my high-school years, a friend dared me to join the dance team. I actually had to audition and ended up making it.'

He went along to the audition for *Glee* as part of their nationwide casting call, ended up singing Nat King Cole's 'L-O-V-E' and the producers looked at his dance videos online. They were impressed by his talent and gave him the role. His other footballer-turned-gleek counterpart is Matt Rutherford, who is played by Dijon Talton, an actor-dancer from California. After starring in a few television commercials with Tyra Banks and in the movie, *L.A. Without a Map* (1998), Dijon can't believe his luck in having landed a role on *Glee*: 'I have always wanted to sing, I have always wanted to act, I've always wanted to dance and I've been doing it since I was a child, on and off.'

Glee is also giving Cory and the guys a crash course in all different kinds of music. 'I listen to everything from death metal to jazz, but there were a lot of R&B songs I wasn't familiar with,' Cory admitted to *TV Guide*. 'And there was a song from Barbra Streisand I didn't know. She's not on my iPod!' So far, his favourite song to have performed on the show is the same as Harry Shum Jr's – 'Somebody to Love' by Queen.

In as much as he doesn't share the same dance and music background of some of the other actors playing the jocks, Cory is undeniably musical. His drumming skills are evidence of that. 'The last place you'd expect to find America's most popular high-school student is on the drums at the Gemini awards backing up Loverboy in Calgary,' wrote the *National Post*. 'However, Cory Monteith, the 27-year-old Canadian *Glee* star, spent this past Saturday evening doing just that.' If he had to choose a song to sing on the show in the future, he would pick Foreigner's 'I Wanna Know What Love Is'.

And Cory might get the opportunity to sing some of his own songs in the future. He told the *Toronto Star* that he signed to Columbia Records and is in the process of making his own album. 'I have a record deal. What the hell is that? I have a [solo] recording contract with Columbia. I mean, seriously. It really doesn't make any sense to me when I think about it. It probably doesn't make sense to a lot of people, if you think about it.'

It will certainly make sense to any of Cory's fans on the show. At the very least, he must be more comfortable singing karaoke now? 'Absolutely! I tore down some Lionel Richie in Victoria, Canada, just a few nights ago. I can finally have fun singing, for the first time in my life!'

CHAPTER TEN
THE CHEERIOS

Every high school has its villains and for those at the bottom of the social food chain, the enemy can only be the army of popular kids who always seem to have it all. At William McKinley High, those popular kids are the Cheerios – the fit, toned and perfectly styled cheerleaders who never seem to be out of their uniforms. Queen Bee is the gorgeous Quinn Fabray, played by Dianna Agron. Quinn's sidekicks are ditzy blonde Brittany (played by Heather Morris) and scheming Latina Santana Lopez (Naya Rivera). None of the girls had much acting experience before joining *Glee* and neither Heather or Naya were cheerleaders in high school! But this hasn't stopped them from playing the deliciously evil mean girls to perfection.

Although Dianna may look the part of the prim celibacy club President with a penchant for bad boys, she was never a cheerleader in high school. In fact, she says, she was not even popular. 'I definitely wasn't cool in high school. I really wasn't,' she insisted to *HitFix*. 'I did belong to many of the clubs and was in leadership on yearbook and did the musical theatre route, so I had friends in all areas, but I certainly did not know what to wear, did not know how to do my hair, all those things.'

Instead her fluid movements on the Cheerios squad are the product of years of dance training. She was born on 30 April 1986 in Savannah, Georgia, but her family moved across the US to San Francisco, California before she began high school. Her dad worked at the San Francisco Hyatt and Dianna grew up having the rule of the roost, an experience that she would draw from in her writing, as we shall soon see. She started dancing at the age of three, doing jazz and ballet, eventually incorporating hip-hop into her routine as she got older. Dianna danced her way through high school and earned some extra money by teaching dance to other kids. In fact, dance taught her a lot of lessons that she brought with her into later life: 'Having a dance background, I became used to rejection at an early age. Dance is very competitive, especially for a sensitive person like me. But I realised it's better not to take it so seriously. If you beat yourself up, it's hard to keep going.'

THE CHEERIOS

After her final year in school, she knew that before anything else, she wanted to try to live her dream: 'I didn't take the typical path and go to college after high school. Instead, I saved up money from teaching dance classes and moved to LA. But my family was so supportive – I never felt pressure from them.' It was the support from her family and friends that gave Dianna the confidence to pursue what can sometimes seem like an impossible dream: breaking into the entertainment industry. But trying to do so was the first step, as she explained: 'I have friends who went to college for one major and haven't applied it, and others who started at jobs that didn't pan out and had to change course. I've learned that the key [to success] is if you can go to work happy. And if it's not the best fit, you can always change direction.'

Dianna is lucky because she has so many avenues to choose from and she was willing to try everything to be a success. First, came bit parts on television shows such as *Shark*, *Close to Home*, *CSI: NY*, *Numb3rs* and recurring roles on *Veronica Mars* and *Heroes*. She also played Harper in a 13 episode comedy series of short films, *It's a Mall World* (2007), which were directed by her *Heroes'* co-star Milo Ventimiglia and also starred *Veronica Mars'* upcoming actor, Sam Huntington.

Yet Dianna is also a talented writer. In 2009, she wrote, directed, produced and starred in a short called *A Fuchsia Elephant*. Just ten minutes long, the film told the story of a young girl called Charlotte Hill who is on the verge of her 18th birthday. Charlotte is challenged to find a unique way to celebrate and so she decides to throw herself the eighth birthday party she was never given by her alcoholic mother. According to the description on *IMDB*: 'The party is an imaginative romp filled with pirates, gypsies and a fuchsia elephant... the best she's ever had.'

Writing is obviously something Dianna enjoys very much. Her short film gave her the confidence to tackle an even larger project: writing an entire screenplay. The idea revolved around a 28-year-old guy who couldn't say 'I love you' and his relationship with three women. Almost as many people attempt to break into screenwriting as acting and it takes a good idea, a ton of talent and a pinch of luck to get a screenplay even looked at by a movie producer, let alone made into an actual film. However, Dianna had made it her personal philosophy never to back down in the face of impossible odds: 'Once a month, try something you don't think you'd be good at. You can find such happy surprises,' she told *Women's Health* magazine. Dianna's own surprise was that her screenplay was optioned by a film company, which means that one day we could see it turned into a movie.

She gathered inspiration for her characters from time spent people watching in her dad's hotel: 'I got to see many walks of life – politicians, athletes, Tony Robbins... It was the ultimate fishbowl.' Her keen observations are part of what makes her a successful writer, and what attracted her to *Glee*. Dianna appreciates that the series doesn't put people into boxes without room to evolve, change or surprise the viewer. She also understands that high school is a complex emotional time in a young person's life and often there's a lot more going on underneath the surface than meets the eye: 'Sometimes with teens, writers or directors – anybody – short-changes them and makes them be simple, simple individuals: you're either the jock or the popular kid or the nerd. They don't show those shades. Everybody has those shades to them. This show, it really expands upon vulnerability and excitement and anger, all the experiences that you probably actually go through in high school.'

When Dianna was sent the pilot of *Glee*, she instantly recognised the script's potential and was excited to audition and be a part of something she really respected. But that didn't mean she wasn't nervous... really, *really* nervous. 'I was nervous out of my mind,' she told *Women's Health* magazine. 'I was sitting in the parking lot thinking, are you going to do this or are you going to walk away?' Eventually she came to her senses and remembered her mantra: you won't get anywhere if you don't try. So she plucked up the courage and headed for the studio to meet the casting director.

She wouldn't have known it at the time but Ryan Murphy and casting director Robert Ulrich were having difficulty in finding someone to fill the role of the head cheerleader. The time to start shooting was fast approaching and they had almost all the roles filled – except Quinn Fabray.

She came into the audition and sang 'Fly Me to the Moon' by Frank Sinatra. Ulrich spotted something in Dianna, but he had one final ask of her. Could she come back with straight hair? 'They told me to come back with straight hair and to dress sexier,' she said. Her solution was to head straight to the nearest Starbucks – where she could guarantee there would be a bathroom – with a new pair of hair straighteners. There, she sat in the bathroom, straightening out the curls from her blonde hair and apologising to all the caffeine-fuelled patrons desperate to use the loo. 'I'm sorry, I have a really important audition that I have to get!' she told them. Making everyone wait paid off in the end: she came back to the studio looking every inch the perfect cheerleader. Ulrich sent a tape of her audition to the producers, who immediately signed off on her as Quinn. Within a week, Dianna was filming in the studio.

Shooting was like nothing she had experienced before on a television set. Despite dancing her entire life, she managed to get injured during her first routine as a cheerleader: 'I slightly hurt myself during the pilot, coming down from one of the stunts. It's better now. I didn't tear something in my knee, but I strained it. Knees are very sensitive, I've learned. It's crazy, because I've been dancing since I was three on my toes and all these things. And you should never say this, but I've never injured myself ever. I'd seen gnarly injuries with dance and all these things. You shouldn't say that, though, because every day is an opportunity to fall, hurt yourself, so that was my experience.' She was always ready to pick herself back up, though, and she loved that every day was a challenge.

Dianna doesn't see much of herself in Quinn and the rest of the cast say she is the sweetest person on set. One major difference between the two girls is that Dianna is Jewish, not the conservative Christian of the character she plays. She told the audience at Comic-Con that her grandmother had issues at first with her wearing a cross all the time, although she was only acting.

After wrapping the shoot for the first 13 episodes, Dianna didn't stop for a rest. She started to pick up roles in various movies, acting alongside some big-name stars. One such gig was *The Romantics*, an indie flick starring Anna Paquin, Katie Holmes and Josh Duhamel, about eight friends from college who reunite for a wedding. Another was *Burlesque* (both 2010), a musical headlined by Cher and Christina Aguilera, about a small-town wannabe singer who gets her big break in a burlesque club. With movie studio execs desperate to snap Dianna up, it won't be long until she gets a starring role herself. For now, she's happy to work within big ensemble casts, which will give her the ability to learn from more experienced actors and perfect her craft.

Perhaps the most endearing side to Dianna is her willingness to be so open with fans on her blog. You can find her blog at http://felldowntherabbithole.tumblr.com. She began it to keep her friends and family in the loop as she left on the *Glee* promotional tour of Australia. After the 13th episode aired, she wrote a heart-warming tribute to her fans:

What wonderful fans we have. Thank you, thank you, from the bottom of my heart. Up until now, I had been striving diligently in my pursuit to become a working actor, and now that that has become a reality, I want to pinch myself each and very day. Deep into my core, I knew that dedication would pay off (although some days took extra effort to remind myself), but couldn't have imagined a year like this!

What a reward this has been. I feel privileged to be a part of this show. And without our fans, we wouldn't have the luxury of coming back to work, and again saying, 'Yes, I am a working actor.' It feels so good. Tonight's episode is a combination of overwhelming emotions on the screen and off. I remember our last day, and feeling at peace. I knew that if we didn't return, we would still have thirteen charmed episodes, and that nobody could take away the joy that I felt while making them. Blood, sweat and tears. It's all there in this one show. We love it so. We love it so.

Heather Morris (Brittany) also felt privileged to be on the show. Her most high-profile television experience before *Glee* had been on the second season of *So You Think You Can Dance* (US version) in 2006. She and her dance partner Ben featured in the audition portion of the show. It was the classic tug-on-your-heartstrings reality TV moment, edited to create the biggest emotional impact. Two teenagers, the best of friends, signed up to audition for *SYTYCD* with hopes of making the Top Ten together. They chatted to host Cat Deeley about their great friendship, their love of dance and how they would support each other even if one of them didn't make it through. Then came the judging time. In front of a panel of judges, a visibly nervous Ben was told he had made it onto the show – elation all round. But Heather wasn't there to share in his excitement – she was in the judging room next, awaiting her own fate. And the votes were 3-2 against: she hadn't made it to the next stage. When she and Ben reunited there were tears, hugs and more tears as Heather's brief flirtation with reality TV fame ended as swiftly as it had begun.

She didn't let the rejection bother her, however, and kept a level head: 'Everything happens for a reason. I wasn't, like, Debbie Downer after. You have to keep that attitude. After I didn't get it, I went home and re-evaluated things and I said, who cares? I'm gonna do something else.'

In reality, this was just the beginning. Heather Elizabeth Morris, born 1 February 1987 in Scottsdale, Arizona, was destined for bigger stages than she could ever dream of. After *SYTYCD*, she appeared as a backing dancer in television shows such as *Swingtown* and *Eli Stone* (both 2008) before landing a major gig as one of the dancers on Beyoncé's tour, *The Beyoncé Experience*. This was an impressive feat for a girl of only 21. She was one half of the pair of dancers who backed up Beyoncé's 'Single Ladies' anthem as the star performed on the *American Music Awards*, *Saturday Night Live*, *The Today Show* and many others. The dance is one of the cultural moments of the noughties and is widely considered the best video dance routine of all time. It required a lot of stamina and precision – with only two dancers and Beyoncé to look at, every step had to be executed perfectly.

And what about *Glee*? Her career had focused on dance so far, although she had made an appearance in the TV show, *Fired Up*. As it turned out, Heather had a very different route into the show from her cast mates. Initially she wasn't brought in to audition at all, rather she was asked to teach the choreography to the 'Single Ladies' dance to the actors. The producers liked her so much, however, that they asked her to fill the spot of the third cheerleader – Brittany, the vacant blonde from the Netherlands (who thought a ballad was a male duck).

She described the experience to the *Buffalo Examiner*: 'I kind of got to meet and interview with Ryan Murphy because I was doing "Single Ladies" at the time and it just so happened that they needed someone to teach the "Single Ladies" dance. I came in to teach it to the actors. The choreographer actually had come over and spoken to me and said well, they're looking for a third cheerleader and come ready and dressed, you'll meet Ryan Murphy. So I came in, did it, and then a week later I got a call from my agency saying that I booked it. It was pretty awesome. I thought I was going to have to read. I was prepared to do a read or sing but nope, I just kind of had to dance and be pretty, that was it.'

Although the Brittany role is relatively small, Heather has proved to be a scene-stealing actress with impeccable comedic timing. The *New York Post* wrote: 'Dancer Heather Elizabeth Morris was brought onto the show to provide back-up for Quinn in both the musical numbers and evil-doing, but over the course of season one her

Cheerio Brittany has emerged as one of the funniest second bananas on TV right now!' In combination with the more wicked and conniving Santana, the two have managed to develop a fan base of their own and have even been given their own 'Brangelina'-style portmanteau. 'While Heather Morris (Brittany) and Naya Rivera (Santana) have had minimal screen time, they've made it count,' said *After Ellen*. 'Heather in particular has brought the laughs as the Cheerio least likely to get a Mensa invitation. Never mind Finn and Rachel – I'm on Team Brittana now.'

Heather doesn't mind playing such a ditzy character but her fans are often surprised to discover she's not so dumb in real life! While teaching dance in Buffalo, a few kids came up to her and said, 'I thought you were so much dumber than you really are. I'm so astonished that you're such a smart girl.' All Heather could say in return was, 'Thanks!'

Naya Rivera, who plays Santana Lopez, arrived on the show by way of a more traditional route. She had already done plenty of work on television shows as a child. Nothing before compared to *Glee*, though and so she was really excited for the audition. 'My manager knows that I like to sing and dance so I was called in. I have always wanted to sing and dance in a TV show so she told me that this show would be perfect for me. So I went and sang in all of the auditions and ended up getting the role.'

THE CHEERIOS

Half-Puerto Rican and a quarter-German, quarter-African American, Naya was born on 12 January 1987. Her mother was a model in Los Angeles and she shared an agent with her parent when she was just a few months old. As a baby, she did commercials for Kmart and when she was four years old, she starred in Eddie Murphy's sitcom, *The Royal Family*, in 1991. By the time she was six, she knew acting was what she wanted to do for the rest of her life.

Still, there was high school to deal with. She didn't enjoy it much and told *Starry Constellation* magazine, 'I definitely wasn't popular in high school.' She didn't participate in any extra-curricular activities but stuck to acting instead. 'I didn't do anything in high school. My mom made me join choir for a couple of weeks freshman year but I didn't like it, so I quit. All I did was go out for auditions and try to get jobs.'

She had plenty of successful auditions and appeared in *8 Simple Rules* and *CSI: Miami,* but like Dianna Agron, Naya had another passion: song writing. She started writing, 'really heavily around 15 years old. I needed an outlet to get things out. I was a big journal logger. I look back at the journals and it is really embarrassing. I like so-and-so, but he doesn't like my stuff.'

Song writing was her way of expressing her musical side and although acting was still her big passion, she was desperately searching for a way to combine the two.

And that was exactly when *Glee* came along. She also remembers hearing that the creator of *Glee* was Ryan Murphy, which made her even more determined to get the role: 'I'm such a huge Ryan Murphy fan because I love *Nip/Tuck*. I love the way he writes and directs. When I found out that this show was created by him, I was floored! I was so excited to be working on it.'

She was offered the part of Santana Lopez, which she snapped up right away. Naya could identify with her character's competitive nature, although she assures audiences that she's not like Naya in every way! 'My least favourite part [of Santana] would be her mean streak. I can be a bit mean at times but not to the point where I ruin people's lives. It is fun to play, though.'

As she wasn't part of the popular crowd in high school, Naya drew on memories of the cliques in her old high school and she also watched plenty of movies to get into character: 'Since I am playing a high-school student, I go back so I can look and draw from all of the girls that would be closest to Santana (if she were a real person). I also watched a bunch of high-school movies and old shows like *Mean Girls* to really get in the zone and feel like a bitchy sophomore.'

But getting into character was only a small part of the preparation that she had to do for the roles. Naya has never worked so hard on a show in her life – and she loves it! 'I have found the pacing challenging, which I love. I'm surrounded all day every day, with people who are as talented as me, if not more. That always strives me to push myself, especially in the dance department. Our dance numbers are really intense, fast and awesome. I've never had to dance like that before. So, I really try and keep up to do the best that I can. It's been really challenging, but it has been really rewarding at the same time.'

One of the reasons why *Glee* works so well is the cast chemistry. It's clear that they all get along really well. For Heather and Naya, the fact that their characters are always together has made them really close friends, and now the girls are such good friends, their characters' relationship seems more realistic! It works both ways. 'We're together 24/7,' said Heather to the *Philippines Inquirer*. 'We're like our characters – we're always together. We relate a lot to each other.'

CHAPTER ELEVEN

NEW DIRECTIONS

When the *Glee* pilot aired on 19 May 2009, directly after the finale of *American Idol*, there was one cast member who would have found the pairing more than a little ironic. When she was only 17, Amber Riley had auditioned for the second season of *American Idol* – four years later, and she was a major singing star in another FOX television show. 'I auditioned for *American Idol* at 17, they told me, "No,"' she recalled. She didn't even get so far as to incur the wrath of Simon Cowell or to be sweetly turned down by Paula Abdul. In fact, she never made it further than singing for the producers of the show.

Like any 17-year-old with the dream of following in

the footsteps of *Idol*'s first winner, Kelly Clarkson, Amber was devastated: 'My life was crushed when they told me "No". But I was 17, it was a long time ago and rejection like that only makes you stronger, gets you asking – how can I better myself?' It just goes to show that there's no use in pinning all your hopes on one audition: if Amber had let the experience overshadow her life, she would never have ended up the star she is today.

One thing's for certain: wherever Amber's path was going to take her, it would involve music. Amber Patrice Riley was born on 15 February 1986 in Los Angeles, California. From a very early age, her mother recognised her musical talent. 'I was actually two years old when mother discovered how much I loved music and how easy it was for me to pick up the songs that she would sing. My first performance was at a park. I just remember singing and a lot of clapping at the end, but I was only four at the time.' It would be hard not to sit up and take notice of a little girl with such a big voice.

All through her time at La Mirada High School, Amber worked hard to make it into the business. She didn't have much time for any school activities such as a Glee Club or high-school theatre. 'I kind of had a life outside of high school,' says the actress. 'I was singing in background, singing in choir, studio work. There wasn't a Glee Club in my school, and if there was, I sincerely apologise, I had no idea.' It was in 2002, when she was

16, that she landed her first role in the pilot of the TV show, *St. Sass*. Although the series was never picked up by a network it featured Ryan Murphy as one of the writers – a connection that was to become hugely important in the future. Her work on *St. Sass* led to a role in *Cedric the Entertainer Presents* (2002), a comedy sketch show.

She might not have been involved in any extra-curricular activities, but Amber definitely remembers her high school as having the same highs, lows, intrigues and excitement of William McKinley High. 'My high school was full of drama, just like that,' she said. 'And I'm happy not to be the only person who went to Melrose Place High School.' She also had a back-up in case she wasn't able to make a career out of acting or singing and attended beauty school for a while although her main goal was to work in the entertainment industry and so she sang at a lot of open mics in Santa Monica, California. She also was no stranger to the stage, performing in *Mystery on the Docks* with the Los Angeles Opera.

Meanwhile, it turned out that the producers were having a lot of difficulty in casting the character of Mercedes Jones, the diva with the powerhouse vocals. The actress who took on the role had to be a triple threat: she must have an incredible singing voice, good rhythm to pick up the dance moves and the acting skills to pull off Mercedes' complex personality and storyline.

Amber didn't really know what to expect when she came to the audition. She knew that she was going to be asked to sing and so she thought it was only a singing role, probably somewhere in the background.

Of course, Ryan Murphy remembered her from the experience of working together on *St. Sass*, but he never realised in that time that she could sing. And not just sing... completely wipe the floor with any competition. Amber revealed the details of her audition on *Up Close with Amber Riley*: 'When I came into the first audition [Ryan Murphy's] mouth dropped and his eyes were wide open when he found out I could sing because he didn't know I could. He asked me to sing a song from *Dreamgirls* and I was completely mortified and terrified because I had never ever sung that song before but ended up having a wonderful time.' That song from the Broadway musical was 'And I Am Telling You I'm Not Going', initially made famous by Jennifer Holliday in 1982 and then revived by Jennifer Hudson in the 2006 movie version with Beyoncé.

Casting director Robert Ullrich remembers knowing right away that Amber was the one. By then, they had heard a few people sing from the role but the actress 'sang literally two lines of ['And I Am Telling You I'm Not Going'] and like, we have Mercedes. It was so exciting! That has got to be one of the most exciting moments that I've ever had in casting.'

Amber was similarly thrilled to realise that she wouldn't just be singing backing vocals, but singing, dancing and acting as one of the co-stars of a musical ensemble. She had found her dream role at least. 'Everything happened so fast and I'm blessed to be a part of something so influential to young people and to be having so much fun living a part of my dream!' she said in an interview with the blog, *Young, Fat, & Fabulous*.

The topic of her size is something Amber is quite willing to talk about. She is now a comfortable size 16 US (18 in the UK), but refuses to be categorised by a label in a clothing store. It wasn't always that way, however. Growing up in California, the pressure to be thin and conform to certain so-called 'standards of beauty' was intense. Amber even thought about putting her Hollywood dreams aside as she struggled with her confidence. 'I actually noticed [the pressure to be thin] more when I was younger which is why I stopped, it was getting to my self-esteem,' she admitted candidly. 'But once I learned I am not my dress size and to never let anyone put me in a box, I was more content with being myself and letting the world see my light shine.'

One of her icons is Queen Latifah, another powerful woman in show business who refuses to let size dictate her success. 'You're not your dress size, you're not your shoe size, you're not your pants size,' Amber told *Life & Style*, proving that she's fast becoming a role model for plus-size girls. 'If I'm going to wear a name tag, it's going to say "Amber Riley", not "Fat Girl"!'

Part of Amber's sassy self-confidence shines through to her performance as Mercedes Jones. And she has to have confidence now, as Mercedes fronts some of the show's biggest numbers. The bring-down-the-house rendition of 'And I Am Telling You I'm Not Going' in 'Sectionals', the final episode notwithstanding, she belts out the female lead in 'Gold Digger' and creates a true smash hit while singing Jazmine Sullivan's 'Bust Ya Windows'. Amber was a big fan of the R&B tune before it was written into the show. As you have already read about earlier in the Hitting the High Notes chapter (page 33), by singing the song on set in between takes, Amber inspired Ryan Murphy to write it into the script. Zach Woodlee's choreography was ambitious for a girl who wasn't the most experienced of dancers, but she pulled it off with style.

'I was nervous when I saw the background dancers for the first time because they're so tall and they're kicking their legs up in the middle. I'm like, my head's gonna be chopped off,' she told the *LA Times*. 'I hadn't danced for a long time but now I'm really comfortable. [P]erforming is what I'm used to. I'm a little more comfortable doing this than the acting part.'

The fantasy sequence where Mercedes sings this song is one of her more vulnerable moments – when she realises that the boy she has a crush on (Kurt), likes someone else. She doesn't quite understand, or perhaps she's unwilling to admit the truth about Kurt's sexuality to herself yet and so the hurt she feels is genuine. She's still struggling with her identity and sees his reaction as a rejection of her – although, of course, it has nothing to do with that. By staying on with New Directions and participating in the Glee Club, however, Mercedes learns more about who she is and so becomes more confident.

Amber never had the experience of a Glee Club in her real high-school days, but she now fully appreciates their value. Not being one to simply rest on her convictions, in late 2009 she took part in VH1's Save the Music Foundation, 'a non-profit organisation dedicated to restoring instrumental music education in American public schools, and raising awareness about the importance of music as part of each child's complete education'. Several high-profile celebrities such as Beyoncé, Kelly Clarkson and Mariah Carey have supported the programme in the past. Amber is passionate about bringing music programmes back into schools, with the hope that music can boost self-esteem and become a great creative outlet for kids without many options.

As for Amber's own career, the options are limitless. Her *Glee* experience would be the perfect segue into musical theatre on Broadway, which is one of her dreams. And to think, it almost ended with one failed reality TV audition. Amber is able to look on the bright side now, though. 'You know what? I still work on FOX and I get paid!' she declared. "Thank you, *American Idol*!'

Someone who had little or no professional acting experience before *Glee* was Chris Paul Colfer, who plays gay soprano, Kurt Hummel. Born on 27 May 1990, Chris was still in his teens while the first season was shot. Like Amber, from an early age he knew that he wanted to perform: 'Since I was an embryo,' he told the *LA Times*.

He might have been singing and dancing in the womb but he didn't get his stage debut until the age of eight, when he played the character Snoopy. 'I saw a light go on in my son that has never turned off,' said his mum, Karyn Colfer. 'We had this child, Christopher, who was extremely gifted in all areas. He was very smart, academically; he was very mature for his age because of his sister's illness, and this was his outlet. It was a way for him to have something that was his very own, and his father and I committed to making sure that he went after this.'

His sister, Hannah, was born with a critical illness which meant that she was constantly in and out of hospital, so Chris often chose to take care of her rather than hang out with people he knew from school.

High school was 'absolutely horrible' in Chris's opinion but he hasn't had much time to put things in perspective! As the youngest cast member of *Glee*, his high-school memories are also the freshest. He attended Clovis East High School in Central California, where he was an active participator in all sorts of extracurricular activities, from debating to drama to being editor of the school's literary magazine. In fact, he was an accomplished debater, winning several Speech & Debate championship titles.

'I was made fun of a lot in high school because of the way I sound and the way I was. I was a lone duck in a swan-filled pond, who criticised everyone so I think everyone might be going, "Oh, he's playing the gay character. Figures." Just because that's how they perceived me.' Just like his character in *Glee*, Chris never allowed the taunts to get in his way, though. He actually cultivated his unique high-sounding voice as he knew it would set him apart from other male vocalists: 'Right when my voice started changing, I would purposely start singing really high songs every day, constantly. Actually, the *Wicked* soundtrack is what I would sing along to the most.'

One of Chris's crowning high-school achievements was writing and performing his own play. He explained his innovative idea to *Advocate*: 'The end of my senior year, my school did this thing for the seniors called *The Senior Show*, where one senior was designated to do whatever he wanted for however much time on the stage

– they get their own show, in a sense. All the other kids previous to me had done SNL-type skits and gags, and that type of stuff but I was dead serious that I wanted to do a show that would be funny and adult, so I wrote this spoof called *Shirley Todd*, which is *Sweeney Todd* except all the roles were gender-reversed, so I was Mr. Lovett rather than Mrs. Lovett, and it took place in modern-day, punk-rock London. It was a lot of fun.'

Very few high-school kids would even audition for a play, let alone have the discipline to sit down and create something entirely new. Chris was obviously a very special kid with an immense future ahead of him.

Of course, by his final year of high school, Colfer was already a seasoned performer in his community theatre. He tried out for every play available and eventually signed with a Hollywood agent, who was also a family friend. With the support of his mum, they travelled back and forth to auditions in L.A., but without much luck.

Knowing how brilliant he is in *Glee,* it's difficult to know why it took over 30 auditions before Chris landed a role. It's not such a mystery to him, though, because he sees auditions as his weakest point: 'I'm horrible at auditions, anyway. Maybe that's why I never got anything – it's my Achilles' heel.'

Eventually, his agent pointed him in the direction of a new musical-comedy show and Chris was intrigued. However, it wasn't the idea of the production that excited him, it was the man behind it. Chris was a huge Ryan Murphy fan before the audition and had watched *Nip/Tuck* religiously. The series covered all sorts of controversial topics and was well known for its graphic depictions of plastic surgeries – not your average viewing for a young teenager. But for Chris, watching the adult TV show was his secret thrill: 'I didn't go through a teenage rebellion period because I saw *Nip/Tuck*. That was my teenage rebellion. My mom would say, "You're not allowed to watch that," blah blah blah.'

The role that Chris tried out for was that of Artie, in the wheelchair. However, he walked into the audition room a nervous wreck and managed to drop his script all over the floor. The number he had prepared was 'Mr. Cellophane' from the musical *Chicago* and he had practised it over and over with his grandma. 'It was very nerve-racking auditioning in front of Ryan Murphy because I'm such a huge fan. It was hard. He's very nice. He's a little intimidating at first, but he's great.'

He needn't have been so nervous, though as Murphy loved him straightaway: 'He's never been formally trained and I just thought he was so talented and gifted and unusual. I've never seen anyone who looks like him or acts like him, or sounds like him. You'd think he'd been at Juilliard for six years but he hasn't.'

143

Indeed, it turned out to be a case of Murphy realising that Chris *had* to be a part of the show. But he wasn't right for Artie. In fact, he wasn't right for any of the roles that Murphy had written thus far, especially not the part that he eventually dropped to play Kurt: 'They got rid of a role called Rashish,' Chris told *New York* magazine. 'Rashish was just like a nerd, but he was everything Kurt was – except he wasn't the gay character, he was genuinely in love with Mercedes. But I guess they didn't really know what to do with it, or where to go with it.'

For Murphy, inspiration struck as he was watching Chris sing his audition. 'Why do I have the feeling you've been Rolf on *The Sound of Music* before?' he asked. 'I know, I have von Trapp written all over me,' replied Colfer, who looked remarkably at ease bantering with his idol in his audition video. 'I actually *was* Kurt in *The Sound of Music* a long time ago.'

Murphy then thanked him for attending and Chris walked out of the audition room, still unsure whether or not he was to be part of the new venture.

GLEEFUL! MOMENT
Kurt's last name 'Hummel' comes from the rosy-cheeked Hummel figurines that Murphy's mother used to collect.

But the audition process wasn't over. His agent was told that Chris was not going to be given the part of Artie but he was asked to try out again, this time for a new role – a character called Kurt Hummel. Chris didn't make the connection properly or perhaps he didn't dare believe his hero would be so impressed as to give him his own role. Even when he was told that he had got a part in *Glee*, he didn't know exactly what it was going to be as the show was still a work in progress. 'I actually had no idea what the role was when I signed the contract 'cause it was still being written. All my original contracts say something ridiculous like "Artie 2,"' he told *New York* magazine. Once everything was finalised, however, Murphy told the agent the truth: that he had written the role especially for Chris. 'I was on cloud nine – cloud 19, actually,' said the actor, and understandably so!

In fact, what Chris had done was to let the *Glee* creator know that he had neglected one very important point of view in the show – Murphy's own. 'When we started auditioning, I thought it was kind of ridiculous that we're doing a musical about kids and expression and we don't have the gay point of view,' Murphy told the *LA Times* and revealed that he had yet to draw on his own experience of being openly gay in high school. Perhaps that's why the character of Kurt is so loved – Murphy has been able to infuse a lot of himself into the part and it rings very true to life, if exaggerated a little for television effect!

One of the most poignant relationships in the show is between Kurt and his dad. Their relationship is loosely based on Murphy's own relationship with his father – accepted with open arms, but not necessarily understood. This was an important message for him to bring to *Glee* and its audience. 'Having a dad that loves you as a young man is a very powerful thing that you carry into the world,' he told the *LA Times*. 'Because no matter what you do: in some weird, unconscious way if you're a guy, you always try to please your dad. I think it's a great thing to put on television. You've seen the gay character that gets kicked out of the house or is beaten up. You haven't seen the gay character that is teased a little bit, but wins and triumphs.'

Kurt was to become that character and with his expensive taste in fashion and witty dialogue, he has won over a myriad of fans. Chris still can't believe his luck that Murphy wrote such a perfect role just for him and is incredibly flattered that he sees in Chris a younger version of himself: 'Everything that's happened I can understand, except for that part. That part is completely mind-blowing. Every time I think of it my eyes get wide and I just can't believe it. It means the world to me because I want to do what Ryan does someday. For him to see me in him, I can't even describe it.'

He is also quick to recognise what a huge honour it is

for him. Chris was never out in high school because he was afraid of the reaction: '[Back home] people still have their "Yes on 8" signs on their front lawns and the election was months ago.' The 'Yes on 8' that he is referring to is the choice to vote 'yes' for Proposition 8, which proposed to restrict the definition of marriage to exclude same-sex couples. Proving that gay marriage is still a hugely contentious issue even in a state dominated by the left-wing entertainment industry, Proposition 8 was voted in. By playing a gay character and coming out as gay himself, Chris is opening the doors for others like him, who are scared of the consequences of being honest with their friends and family. 'It's challenging, but right now I couldn't care less – I think it's done such good things for kids out there,' he admits. It's a big task for such a young man, but Chris has already proved himself more than up to it.

GLEEFUL! MOMENT

Chris has nicknamed his fans the 'Kurtsies'.

He told *New York* magazine: 'I think out of everyone, I get the biggest range of fan letters. I get people saying they love the character and the show, but also people telling me their coming-out stories – like, when they told their parents or their wife and four kids.'

And it wasn't the only time when Chris was to influence the direction of the show. He remembers telling one of his high-school horror stories on set: about a time when he tried to sing in the school's talent show but the teachers wouldn't let him sing 'Defying Gravity' from *Wicked* because it's a female number. 'I was sort of venting about it to [Murphy],' he told *Advocate* magazine. Murphy then wrote the story into an episode and Chris eventually got to perform the song to millions of viewers around the world.

So there's a lot of Chris in Kurt: 'I've gone from a theatre geek in high school to a theatre geek on national television!' But Chris doesn't share his character's love of fashion – his favourite place to shop is Target, a discount clothing retailer. He also thinks that Kurt is much more popular than he was in high school, even with the occasional Slushie!

Stuttering goth Tina Cohen-Chang couldn't be more different from Jenna Noelle Ushkowitz, the bubbly Broadway veteran from Long Island, New York. She was born on 28 April 1986 in Seoul, South Korea, before being adopted as a baby by Brad Ushkowitz.

Jenna was a precocious child who loved playing up for the cameras. She got into show business from as early as three years old: 'I was kind of one of those kids who would go up to people in restaurants and say hi to all the tables – that kind of thing,' she told JustJared.com. 'So it kind of rooted from that and they were, like, why don't you get her into modelling? She's a cute little Asian girl! So they put me in and we found a manager on Long Island. The first job that I booked was Fisher-Price for the Dress-Me-Up Ernie doll and the second one was a Toys R Us commercial with Geoffrey the giraffe.' Jenna also went on to do three Jell-O commercials with Bill Cosby.

Her first taste of the musical theatre industry was at the age of nine when she played a role in *The King & I* on Broadway. Her vocal talent was quickly recognised in the industry and by the age of 13, she had the huge honour of singing the national anthem at a Knicks' game in Madison Square Garden. Her parents were keen for her to get a good education, however, and she attended Long Island's Holy Trinity Diocesan High School. The school is well known for its performing arts programme – the Trinity Theatre Academic Program. For this, students must audition separately from their admission to the high school. In 2001, the theatre programme staged the world's first high-school production of *Les Misérables*, which Jenna was a part of. She also joined her school's show choir, which helped to develop her singing voice.

After high school, Jenna went on to Marymount Manhattan College and minored in musical theatre. It was then that she knew she wanted to go back to Broadway. She joined the ensemble of the new musical

Spring Awakening, which starred her future *Glee* cast mate Lea Michele. Jenna understudied for the parts of Anna, Martha, Thea and Ilse.

She was still working on Broadway when one of the casting associates for *Glee*, Jim Carnahan, was sent to New York to scout out talent. All the young actors in *Spring Awakening* were brought in to audition for a role and Jenna read for the part of Tina.

The challenge in the auditions for *Glee* was that Murphy hadn't fully worked out a background to each of the characters, and so he asked each person auditioning to make one up. Jenna's plan was to give Tina a really deliberate stutter. 'Did she have Tourette's?' Murphy asked her and he seemed a little sceptical of Jenna's performance. 'I walked out of that audition and said, "I didn't get that",' Jenna recalled. She should have had more faith, though, as she was called back. 'I went in for a day and I tested for network, and Tina just kinda happened from there.'

The Tina we know and love now has a much subtler stutter and she is also very shy. Jenna tried to break down the stereotype of the depressed goth by recognising that Tina isn't unhappy, she's hasn't yet broken out of her shell. 'I think she's got a lot of layers – people may say, "Oh, she's the gothic one, she's not going to be happy," but I think there's a lot of happiness underneath.' It's Glee Club that gives Tina a big boost in confidence: when she's singing, she becomes a different person. Of course, the fact that she has faked the stutter all along is just proof of the insecurity that is slowly disappearing. Although it's a heartbreaking moment when Tina admits her big lie to Artie, the underlying message is that she no longer requires the security blanket of a speech impediment to make her unique.

Even more than halfway through the season, Ryan Murphy still hasn't revealed Tina's background, so Jenna has to make it up. She's moved on a long way from the girl with Tourette's, though: 'In my mind, I think she's rebelling against her mother, who's this Asian feminist. Tina's almost always smiling but I think she's angry, deep down. She's also really shy, but the Glee Club is helping her slowly come out of her box.'

The transition from stage to screen has also been challenging, but a challenge Jenna has relished. She recognises the differences between the two types of performance art: 'I have to say, as a theatre-trained actor, there is nothing like Broadway/live theatre. I love the instant response and energy from the audience. TV is a completely different world and I'm pretty new to it, so I'm enjoying learning new things every day – but *Glee* is the ultimate dream, because we get to do both!'

Like a lot of the cast who got their start in theatre, she still hears the call when it comes to treading the boards. 'I am loving doing television, but theatre is where my training is and I would love to come back,' she told *Theater Mania*. There's one role in particular that Jenna is really gunning for: 'I am hoping they'll do a Broadway revival of *Miss Saigon* – and I've been pushing and pushing to be seen for the film version. I actually finally got to meet Lea Salonga [who originated the role of Kim in *Miss Saigon* in 1992] the other day and it turns out she loves *Glee*. That was so exciting!'

Television can also have its dangers, as Jenna discovered one day on set: 'I got whacked on my hand when I was doing "Don't Stop Believin'". It was this huge bruise on the bone, it was so bad. Physically, I am afraid of the camera because we have to dodge it and then sometimes it'll be on somebody [else] so you have to keep dancing in case they get your hand, but at the same time, you're like making funny faces at the person who's on camera.'

One of Jenna's best friends on the set – and probably the one she's making the most funny faces at – is Kevin Michael McHale, who plays Artie Abrams, the guitar-playing, glass-wearing boy in a wheelchair.

Kevin was born on 14 June 1988 in Plano, Texas. Like Chris, his memories of high school are still fresh: 'I didn't belong in a clique or group, I was totally neutral.' School was a necessity, rather than something he enjoyed: he attended only as much as was required and did absolutely nothing extracurricular. He blames his work, as he was already hard at work, acting and singing.

NEW DIRECTIONS

One aspect of this work was his boy band NLT (Not Like Them). He joined the group of four when he was just 14 years old. The other members of the band were Travis Garland, Justin Joseph Thorne (JJ) and Vahe Sevani (V). Although the experience was short-lived, the band did have some success. They signed up to Chris Stokes' label TUG Entertainment in 2006. Perhaps most importantly, Kevin got to work with some of the industry's big names right from the start, experience which would eventually help him feel much more comfortable in the *Glee* recording studios: 'I was in a boy band... Eventually we started recording an album. We worked with Timbaland and Pharrell and stuff, so we got to work with a lot of great people. We went on tour with the Pussycat Dolls.'

The group also released a single – 'That Girl' – on 13 March 2007. A couple of years later, though, and they split up after running into difficulties during the release of their debut album. A few of tracks were leaked onto the internet and the label subsequently dropped its support.

Just as every cloud has a silver lining, Kevin realises that he could not have asked for better preparation for *Glee* than being in a boy band: 'It was a really great learning experience, especially for *Glee,* because it was the recording, the rehearsals, I would have no idea if it wasn't for that. So now I'm not scared, nervous. I didn't expect to sing Freddie Mercury, that's terrifying, but at least I'm not scared about the recording part.'

He wasn't new to acting either. In 2007, Kevin appeared as a pizza delivery boy in the American version of *The Office*, with Steve Carell. A year later, he also landed a role on the popular vampire TV series, *True Blood*, where he played a coroner's assistant. In fact, he went into his part on *True Blood* without knowing anything about the show: 'I didn't know what *True Blood* was at the time, and the audition was like three words or something, but I didn't really like vampires. I had no idea that I would be back for more than one episode.'

The bit parts in TV that he had already achieved convinced Kevin that he wanted to stick to acting over pursuing his music career, with NLT or otherwise. He managed to obtain a copy of the *Glee* script and he knew then that he had to audition: 'I had never laughed out loud reading anything script-wise before.'

The audition process was intense, especially as Artie was one of the first characters to be auditioned for. As he was sitting outside the audition room, waiting for his name to be called, Kevin remembers it being extremely awkward because he could hear the other candidates through the walls. Still, he tried not to let his nerves get to him. He had prepared a song, 'Let It Be' by The Beatles, but he only learned the first verse and chorus as he thought he would be asked to keep it short. 'Halfway through the song they said, "Keep singing", but I didn't know the words... it was just bad,' he revealed.

It couldn't have gone that badly because he was offered the part, although Kevin admits that the nerves probably helped him play a convincing Artie: 'I was the first Artie they saw. I was a nervous wreck. I think the nervousness helped because I intentionally pushed that into Artie so he was like, hyperventilating all the time.'

It was probably *Glee*'s most controversial casting decision. A lot of disability rights groups wished the show had chosen an actor who uses a wheelchair in real life. There are very few roles available to disabled actors and it seemed unfair that the part went to an able-bodied person. And yet, the casting team for *Glee* were given very specific directives: to find the absolute best person for the role, no matter what.

'We brought in anyone: white, black, Asian, in a wheelchair,' explained Brad Falchuk to the *Associated Press*. 'It was very hard to find people who could really sing, really act, and have that charisma you need on TV.'

Kevin now finds that many fans are surprised to see him walking around – they expect to see him in a wheelchair. He tries to take the controversy in his stride: 'You know, I'm just doing my own take on it. It wasn't up to me whether or not I got the role – I can only do my part and if the producers liked me for it, great. Usually when you audition, there's a character breakdown with their ethnicity on it and whatever, but with *Glee*, there wasn't. It didn't say that Tina had to be

Asian – they wanted a diverse cast but whoever was right for the part got it. From my understanding, actors in wheelchairs did audition, but luckily they felt I was right for Artie.'

The episode 'Wheels' really brought the issue to the forefront as the entire New Directions group were put in wheelchairs. They had to learn the hard way exactly what it was like to spend time in a wheelchair – and they learnt from the best. Aaron Fotheringham, an extreme wheelchair athlete, was brought in to be Kevin's stunt double for the episode. An inspiration to the whole cast, Aaron is best known for being the first person to perform a backflip in a wheelchair, which he did at the age of 14.

Kevin enjoyed watching his fellow cast mates having a hard time: 'It's really funny because no one else had used a wheelchair before, so Amber [Riley] fell off the ramp, Lea [Michele] had a demon wheelchair and everyone was dying. I hadn't realised how much I'd learned about using one until I kinda had to teach everyone to learn forward while going up a ramp so they didn't fall out!'

It's the fact that *Glee* gets people talking about these controversial issues – from homosexuality to disabled actors, deaf choirs to cheerleaders with Down's syndrome – that makes the show so important at the moment. It's a programme that's not afraid to do something different, and that's unique in television. The gratification that the cast receive from people coming up to them and saying: 'Thank you for playing us on TV, the outcasts, the weirdos, the losers' makes it all worthwhile. And who hasn't felt left out of high school or any other social network at some point in their lives? *Glee* is a show for everyone – and the cast is a reflection of that.

CHAPTER TWELVE
THE CHEERIOS' SERIAL KILLER

'Jane Lynch is the star of the show, let's not kid ourselves,' laughs Cory Monteith. And he couldn't be more right. With her turn as the track-suited Glee Club-hating, foul-mouthed cheerleading coach Sue Sylvester, she manages to steal every scene she's in. Critics and audiences alike adore her for her deadpan delivery of some of the show's most hilarious lines. But how do you sum up an incredible career that has spanned over 30 years and hundreds of different TV and film roles?

Time for a little Sue Sylvester advice: 'You think that's hard? Try living with hepatitis!' she snaps in the pilot episode.

Right from the very beginning, Jane Lynch knew that

she was going to be an actress. 'I came out of the womb wanting to perform and act,' she told *Oprah* magazine. 'I was not one of those people who kind of debated back and forth about what I wanted to do when I grew up. I knew what I wanted to do.' She was born on 14 July 1960 in Dolton, Illinois – a suburb of Chicago – to a housewife mother and a banker father. Most of her teenage years were spent drinking and listening to her parent's stories: 'This is going to make my parents sound *terr-i-ble*, but all through high school, we were the drinking house. We'd sit around the kitchen table with my parents and drink beer.'

She attended Thornridge High School, where she was an active member of the school choir. Even though she knew she wanted to be an actor, she just didn't feel comfortable participating in her school's amateur dramatic productions. Her sole venture onto the theatre scene was in a one-act play, but she backed off at the last moment: 'I got so scared because I knew this was what I wanted to do with my life,' she told the *Guardian*.

And she explained the consequences still further in the *New York Times*: 'I got a reputation at my little high school for being a quitter and I didn't get in a play for the rest of my high-school career. I mean, I got little parts here and there but I wasn't able to shine because nobody trusted that I would stay in it. I auditioned for everything and I got turned down. Oh, it was terrible. So

Hype for *Glee* reaches fever pitch as several of the cast members embarked on 'The Gleek Tour' in the summer of 2009 to meet fans and sign autographs.

Above: The young cast members huddle together at a *Glee* press conference.

© *Ian Daniels/ Rex Features*

Below: Answering audience questions and enjoying the spotlight during the Fox Network portion of the 2009 Summer Television Critics Association Press Tour.

© *Getty Images*

Above: There were plenty of rumours surrounding whether Lea Michele and Cory Monteith were a couple in real life.

© Sara Jay/ Rex Features

Left: Their characters may be at opposite ends of the William McKinley High social spectrum but Lea and Dianna Agron are great friends and roommates.

© Humberto Carreno/ Rex Features

The cast give photographers the 'L' for Loser sign – the universal calling card for *Glee*.

Clockwise from above left: Jayma Mays, Jessalyn Gilsig, Patrick Gallagher and Naya Riviera.

Above: Mark Salling, Dijon Talton, Jane Lynch and Harry Shum Jr pose for a photo-op.
© *Rex Features*

Below left: They don't just work together – they're also great friends! Kevin McHale and Jenna Ushkowitz.
© *Getty Images*

Below right: Two of the Cheerios and their coach: Heather Morris and Naya Riviera with Jane Lynch.
© *Rex Features*

Above: Kevin McHale, Jenna Ushkowitz and Chris Colfer get into the loser-spirit.

© *Getty Images*

Below: Mark Salling, Amber Riley and Cory Monteith together at the 'Carol-Oke Contest' in December 2009.

© *Sarah Jaye/ Rex Features*

Glee has benefited from a number of guest stars – and more keep signing up to join the cast of this amazing show.

Above left: Kristin Chenoweth is a Broadway superstar.

Above right: Idina Menzel is another Broadway legend who is joining the cast as the coach of 'Vocal Adrenaline', McKinley High's biggest competition.

Below left: Madonna is letting *Glee* use her entire catalogue of music to create an all-Material Girl episode.

Below right: Soon to be joining Jane Lynch in 'getting physical' is pop legend Olivia Newton-John.

A People's Choice Award caps off an incredible year for the entire *Glee* team and there are no signs of slowing down for this phenomenal hit show!

© *Getty Images*

I vowed I would never walk away from it again.' If there was a lesson to be learned, it was a good thing that it happened so early on in her career.

Apart from missing out on being one of the stars of her high-school theatre programme, Jane has good memories of high school and doesn't remember being part of any cliques. She hung around the fringe of the social groups, flitting from one to the next, without settling anywhere in particular: 'I was one of those happy travellers and really didn't stay in one group. I kind of got around without getting humiliated and was in a little bit of everything. I knew some of the popular kids, I knew the theatre dorks, choir kids (I loved choir) and smoked cigarettes with the burnouts and the woodshop people. I got around.' That may have been because the other kids were afraid of including her, though. She claims to have earned the nickname 'the Narc' in high school – more for her innocent ignorance than any similarity to the narcotics police – and told *TV Addict*: 'I was very naïve. People were having sex and doing drugs and I had no idea. In fact, my nickname behind my back was "the Narc." I'd walk into a party and hear whispers of "the Narc's here."'

Jane left Thornridge to attend Illinois State University, where she enrolled as a Mass Communications major because her mother wanted to make sure that she ended up with a proper job. She couldn't keep the acting bug under wraps for very long, however. 'By the end of my freshman year, I was a full-on theater major,' she told *Oprah* magazine. 'I changed my major, and I don't think I even bothered to tell anybody.'

It was while attending Illinois State that she met the teacher who was to become the inspiration for Sue Sylvester. She was 'referred to as the "Dragon Lady". [She] kind of taught by humiliation and fear, and was held up as this great god of acting,' Jane told *America's People* magazine. 'That's kind of the Sue Sylvester equivalent for cheerleading.' Unfortunately, that influential teacher isn't alive today to see Jane perform and she would surely have been proud of her student's success – although Jane might have kept her influence a secret!

Jane received her bachelor's degree in theatre and went on to complete her Master of Fine Arts at Cornell University. The theatre-training programme was small, with only six other students in the class, and she credits her Masters with opening her eyes to her own range. With so few students for every play, Jane was heavily involved in all the performances: 'I was stretched to within an inch of my life and it really revealed that I had more talent than I thought I did. It was like boot camp: whatever you have rises to the surface. I played ingénues, I played old ladies; I learned how to fence, to dance, to sing.'

It was always comedy, though, where she felt most comfortable. After receiving her Masters, she moved from Cornell University to Chicago, where she joined the improvisational comedy troupe, The Second City, and worked with the Steppenwolf Theatre Company. The Second City is famous for nurturing many of the best comedians in Hollywood today and has become a seemingly endless source of comedic talent for popular sketch shows such as *Saturday Night Live*. Famous Second City alumni include Mike Myers (of *Austin Powers* fame), Steve Carell (*The 40 Year Old Virgin*) and Tina Fey (*SNL, Mean Girls*).

In 1991, she signed up to star in *The Real Live Brady Bunch*, a show re-enacting some of the actual *The Brady Bunch* episodes live on stage. Jane played the part of stay-at-home mum and Brady matriarch, Carol Brady. The show proved to be a massive – and unexpected – success: 'It turned into this big cult phenomenon, and we went to New York for eight months, and then LA for seven months.'

Her extensive background in improvisation helped her become every director's dream: an actress with a smart, quick mind who could roll with the punches and was prepared for anything that came her way. 'Flying by the seat of your pants is what you learn doing *Second City* and *The Real Live Brady Bunch*. It's being open to things not going like you thought they were going to be, and to be able to flow with that and roll with that. You never knew what was going to happen, and that was part of the fun too,' she told *Oprah* magazine.

Indeed, *The Real Live Brady Bunch* gave Jane the necessary exposure to break into the Hollywood market and she landed her first movie role in the 1993 Harrison Ford movie, *The Fugitive*. The experience gave her the confidence to move to Los Angeles to try and carve out a name on the big (or small) screen. Her acting credentials – and the helping hand of a savvy agent – meant that she landed jobs almost immediately. She did anything and everything, from sitcoms to commercials to voiceover work. 'I felt successful all the time – even though nobody knew who I was,' she told the *Guardian*.

The multi-talented Jane even tried her hand at writing. In 1998 she penned the award-winning play, *Oh Sister, My Sister,* in which she also starred. The comedy saw her play a wide range of women journeying through the 'murky waters of feminine discovery'. It earned the Best Comedy Ensemble of the Year Award from *LA Weekly* and was revived in 2004 to kick off the Lesbians in Theater programme at the LA Gay and Lesbian Center.

It's hard to think now that Jane might not have gone much further than bit parts in sitcoms and commercials selling Frosted Flakes. Her agent used to say that she'd 'take any job for a steak and $1.50'. But, like many actors, she was just happy to be doing what she loved for a living. '[Did I ever think] that was it? Yeah, I thought that was it. Believe me, I jumped up and down every time I got one of those roles, but there was a point where I thought: this might be my swan song, this "Empty Nest" episode. And I wasn't real happy with that, but I was also doing voiceover and I was making a living.'

It's also a lesson for every actor that you never know when your big break might be just around the corner. For Jane, one of those Frosted Flakes TV commercials just happened to be directed by comedy genius Christopher Guest.

In the commercial, Jane and fellow actor Sean Masterson play a slightly deranged couple obsessed with Tony the Tiger. They wait anxiously outside the Kellogg's headquarters in the hope of catching a glimpse of the *gr-r-r-eat* cartoon character. Of course, a small animated version of Tony sneaks out behind them without them noticing. It was silly, but the two actors completely improvised the dialogue – and that impressed Guest: '[A]bout six months later, I was at a restaurant in Beverly Hills and Chris walked in and we kind of locked eyes, and he said, "Oh, hi, good to see you. I'm working on a movie, why don't you come by my office today?" And by the end of the day I had the role in *Best of Show*. It was kind of a happy accident.'

Guest is known for his movies, which rely heavily on the improvisational skills of his actors. Along with Canadian writing partner Eugene Levy, he devised a series of films known as 'mockumentaries' – fictional comedies styled as documentaries. Together they would write storylines and character backgrounds for each scene on cards and leave the actors to improvise, the aim being to achieve a more natural dialogue in this way.

In New York's *Daily News* he explained his method: 'The actors know what the intention of the scene is, but there are no lines written down, and the first time you hear it and see it on the screen, that's it – that's the first time it was said. I've tried to make all these analogies to what we're doing, mostly with music. Like in jazz – there are no music stands. Where's the music coming from? They're making it up. And in these films, this is jamming. This is actor jamming.'

Jane became one of Guest's staple 'jammers' and appeared in his movies *Best in Show* (2000), *A Mighty Wind* (2003) and *For Your Consideration* (2006). She loves acting in comedies: 'I think if you can do comedy, you can do anything, because you can pick up the ironies in life better. It takes a little more investigation into your own heart with comedy; I think you can get away with a lot more in drama. I think you'll find that a good actor usually does comedy really well.'

She also credits Guest with launching her career. 'The man changed my life,' she admits. 'He blew the doors open for me.'

One of those doors was television. Her roles are too numerous to name but she's enjoyed guest appearances on *Arrested Development*, *Criminal Minds* and *Gilmore*

Girls. One of her most memorable performances was on *The L Word*, a drama series portraying the lives of a group of lesbian, bisexual and transgender people. She played a civil rights lawyer and the part was written for her after she admitted that she would take a role in the show 'in a New York minute'.

This was an especially important part for Jane as she had publicly come out as gay a few years earlier, when she was 31. It had been an announcement that had been a long time coming, but she didn't make it immediately known to her parents: 'I didn't want to be gay. I wanted to be... I wanted an easy life. And you know what? I am gay and I still have an easy life.' In fact, in high school – harking back to her nickname as 'the Narc' – she didn't even know what being gay was: 'We used the word "queer" when someone was weird – when I finally heard what it really meant, my heart sank, and I thought, Oh God, that's me.'

She made no secret of her disappointment as voters across America rejected the legalisation of gay marriage and made a public call to the US President, Barack Obama, to take a stand. 'Shouldn't there be safeguards against the majority voting on the rights of a minority?' she said to the *Guardian*. 'If people voted on civil rights in the 60s, it would have never happened. It took somebody like [President] Lyndon Johnson going, "F all of you! I'm going to do this." Obama won't do it. He's a huge disappointment to me.'

The issue has become especially poignant for Jane – she looks set to marry her long-term girlfriend, psychologist Dr. Lara Embry. They want to tie the knot after the airing of the last nine episodes of *Glee* in the US, in May 2010. In 2009, Embry won a National Centre For Lesbian Rights' Justice Award for her involvement in a high-profile custody battle with her former partner.

In 2005, Jane was celebrated as one of *POWER UP*'s 10 Amazing Gay Women in Showbiz and it was there that she met Ilene Chaiken, executive producer of *The L Word*, which led to her landing the role on the hit show.

While many actors struggle with being 'out' in Hollywood, Jane has never faced much adversity in her professional career: 'I think if I were an ingénue – if I were Kate Winslet – it probably would hurt my career, but because I'm Jane Lynch and I'm a character actor, the world isn't projecting their romantic fantasies on me.' In fact, her movie career has been booming. She starred to much acclaim in *The 40 Year Old Virgin (2005)* opposite Steve Carell, whom she knew back in her *Second City* days. Of her co-star, she said: 'He's a very normal, kind of boring guy! Even when we were crazy, working in plays in Chicago in my 20s, he was always very sane, normal. He was the nicest guy in the room and a great improviser. He had heart and vulnerability and a weird self-consciousness, which was so endearing. And he blew up and became a huge star.' She can spotted in almost every comedy of the decade, from *Talladega Nights: The Ballad of Ricky Bobby* to *Role Models*, to *Alvin and the Chipmunks*.

In 2009, Jane got to work opposite one of her idols, Meryl Streep, playing her sister in *Julie & Julia*. They had met once before on the set of *Lemony Snicket: A Series of Unfortunate Events* and Jane remembers being blown away by her then: '[Meryl] hugged me, then she gave me a kiss and told me she was a huge fan of *Best in Show*. And you know, I didn't expect that at all. I was prepared to bow at her feet, so for her to do that was just incredible. And she *held my hand* while we talked. I remember watching *Sophie's Choice* in graduate school and being just *devastated* by her, by that kind of acting. So, for her to do that – to *me*, it was a huge moment for me. It was almost too incredible.'

This time they were on a level playing field and despite her nerves, Jane easily managed to hold her own. There were even whispers of a Best Supporting Actress Oscar nod, although her appearance in the film was a little too brief to be considered.

By any estimation, her stock had gone flying through the roof. There was no need to work for a steak and some spare change anymore. Well, at least now she's asking for a better cut of meat! 'I'm holding out for the porterhouse. I've reached an age when I realise that it's all about valuing yourself.'

That statement just about sums Jane Lynch up perfectly: witty, self-deprecating and modest to a fault about her remarkable achievements. But it would be her next project that was to finally give her the widespread acclaim and time in the spotlight that she deserved.

Ryan Murphy initially conceived the character of Sue Sylvester as a guest spot, not a central character. An episode of *Glee* without Sue is practically impossible to imagine now, but it could have been. In fact, Jane was already contracted to do a pilot for a new show called *Never Better* with a rival US television network, ABC. Fortunately for *Glee*, *Never Better* never got off the ground, and so she was free to become a regular. And thank goodness!

The character of Sue Sylvester instantly appealed to Jane. She was familiar with playing that kind of authoritarian, strong, powerful woman role: 'There is something about being six foot tall and a woman that inspires an authority that I'm not even really asking for. I'll find sometimes that I'll be at a party and I start speaking and everything goes quiet and I'll see people listening to me like I'm an authority. Inside I'm like, "Why are you listening?" But that's how people respond to me. With Julia Roberts, we project our hopes and dreams of that princess character, the ingénue, and she might not be asking for that in real life, but we make her that for us. So I think I might be almost the fairytale evil godmother to people.'

Never before had she got to play a woman in authority so deliciously evil, though. 'Sue is like the culmination of all the power-abusive people I've played. She could be viewed as almost pure evil. Hopefully you're laughing at her, too. She really wraps herself around how mean she can be. She'll walk by a kid with books and knock them down, just to knock them down.'

Jane described the creative process to the *New York Times*: 'Ryan [Murphy] and Ian Brennan and Brad Falchuk took their inner mean girl and created Sue Sylvester... I get to say the most heinous things.' And she doesn't have any trouble bringing all of those 'mean girl' attributes to the surface. In fact, she thinks there's probably a little bit of Sue Sylvester in all of us – it's just that generally we try to suppress those feelings rather than letting them take over: 'She's contemptuous and vengeful, and I've felt that way, but I certainly don't act on it. I have more of a desire to be kind and compassionate than I do to be an awful, humiliating person like Sue can be. But I enjoy the fact she embraces that part of her. I don't embrace that part – I squash it.'

About as iconic as Sue Sylvester's lines are her Adidas tracksuits, which she appears to own in every colour under the sun! 'It's a lot of fun... It's like slipping into your pyjamas when you go to work – I love it.' The tracksuit is the green light for putdowns, in Jane's opinion: 'When I put on that tracksuit I have a licence to say anything I want'.

Whereas most of the other actors had to have significant singing and dancing backgrounds, the same can't be said for Jane. But it wasn't for lack of talent that she had never sung a great deal professionally before, rather a lack of opportunity. *Glee* was finally providing that outlet for her: 'It's kind of a dream come true, because I love to sing. I got to record some singing in the film *A Mighty Wind*, so I had done it before. But it's not as easy as you think. You have to be right on it with the pitch and the timing, and I always thought I was very good at those things, but apparently I'm not.' The first 13 episodes still don't have much singing for Jane but there are rumours that the last nine will do so. She might even get the opportunity to sing 'Physical' with one of her former crushes as a child, Olivia Newton-John.

Learning to dance, however, was another story and she *does* dance in the first few episodes – with Matthew Morrison (Will Schuester) in Episode 8, 'Mash-Up'. This was something in which she had zero experience: 'Gosh, dancing is the biggest challenge. Everything else I just kind of flow into and it's fun. Dancing is the thing I have to work at 10 times harder than everybody else.'

Dancing and singing might not be her strongest suits,

but she plays Sue Sylvester to perfection. Yet Sue isn't the character with whom Jane identifies most. Rather surprisingly, she sees more of herself in the quiet Asian girl with a stutter, Tina Cohen-Chang: 'She's quiet. She stands in the back, and when you hear her sing, you're like, "Oh my gosh! Where did she come from? She has talent." I was kind of that person. I was kind of in the background, and then, every once in awhile, I'd pop in and people would be like, "Where did you come from?"'

She might have been relegated to the background for most of her career – albeit a scene-stealing background, but now she was front and centre. And she was about to be recognised for her hard work by the awards circuit.

On 15 December 2009, Jane received a Golden Globe nomination for Best Supporting Actress in a Series, Miniseries, or Television Film. She told *Hollywood Insider* how she found out: 'I woke up to several messages – when I saw the volume of them, I knew it was probably good news. My agent called me three times and was like, "Get up, get up!" and, you know, I was kind of playing too-cool-for-school and slept through it because I didn't want to get too excited about anything. But this is really a lovely dream. It was so fun to come to work this morning. The kids are beside themselves with excitement, it's great.' The show itself also received a nomination for Best Series (Musical or Comedy).

Her character might not be used to dressing up but Jane

enjoyed the opportunity to dress for the red carpet as a nominee. She didn't fuss over her choice of outfit, though: 'I found a dress for the Golden Globes almost immediately. I went to a designer and he had this dress on a mannequin that I ended up choosing. It took me, like, a moment.' Her choice was a shimmery olive-green ball gown by Ali Rahimi. At the awards themselves, she lost out to Chloë Sevigny, who won for her role as Nicky Grant in *Big Love*, the drama about Mormon polygamy.

She did win the Satellite Award for Best Supporting Actress, however. Jane responded in typical 'Sue Sylvester'-style: 'When you get singled out, you're supposed to say, "Oh it's all about the ensemble," but you know? It's all about *me*, damn it! I won this fucking thing!'

Her sudden rise to fame has swiftly garnered her more respect at home as well. And it's the recognition from her family – more than the views of a panel of awards judges – that really means something to her: 'When I was home for Christmas in Chicago, my family were beside themselves and when I see how excited they are, it kind of kicks in for me. In a way, I've peaked in the last year and I'm really grateful for it. It's one of those things where you think, Well, I can die now if I had to.'

It seems Jane now has it all – and she wouldn't swap her *Glee*-ful life with anybody: 'I love my life; I've got the best life. I think people should want mine!'

CHAPTER THIRTEEN
GUEST STARS GALORE!

Part of *Glee*'s charm and success revolves around its ability to attract megawatt guest stars. Now that 13 episodes have aired, everyone in Hollywood seems to be trying to get in on a *Glee*-ified musical number. Every week there's news of some celebrity – from J. Lo to Justin Timberlake to Madonna the Queen of Pop herself – who's rumoured to be making an appearance. And who wouldn't want to be a part of the happiest show on earth?

The first taste of guest-star magic came with Episode 3, 'Acafellas'. Victor Garber, of *Titanic* and *Alias* fame and a proficient singer and dancer in his own right, was introduced as Will Schuester's dad while the accomplished Broadway actress Debra Monk plays his mum. John

Lloyd Young, a Tony Award-winning actor, joined the cast for a brief role as Henri St. Pierre, the wood-shop teacher, who cuts off his thumbs. But it was Josh Groban's cameo at the end of the Acafellas' performance of 'I Wanna Sex You Up' at the end of the episode that received the most press. Audiences loved seeing the multi-platinum singer-songwriter gently poke fun at his own celebrity, not taking himself too seriously. It was a side to him they hadn't seen before, although there was some disappointment that the 'You Raise Me Up' singer didn't join the Acafellas in some smooth harmonies.

'[The episode] was a little random,' observed *Entertainment Weekly*, 'but it's all worth it for the scene when Groban was hitting on Will's mom. "Josh Groban loves a blousy alcoholic." Hilarious.'

'Most fun of all is a guest appearance by Josh Groban,' said the *New York Times Art Beat* blog. For his part, Josh loved the role. 'I play myself, but I'm definitely acting,' he told the *New York Daily News*. 'I had to play a real jerk version of myself, so it was a lot of fun. I had to serve one of the teachers a restraining order.' Cory Monteith neatly summed up his view: 'Josh Groban refers to Josh Groban as "Josh Groban"... That's kind of an indicator of his character.'

The next episode to feature a prominent guest star, Episode 5 'The Rhodes Not Taken', was an even bigger success. Broadway superstar Kristin Chenoweth burst onto the scene as former McKinley High Glee Club number April Rhodes. It was also the first time *Glee* had a guest star sing the major numbers with the rest of the cast and her 'battle' with Lea Michele is one of the highlights of the entire season.

Kristin was born Kristi Dawn Chenoweth on 24 July 1968 – she added the 'n' to her first name when her opera teacher told her that it would sound more classical. She made her Broadway debut in the musical *Steel Pier* (1997), went on to win a Tony Award for *You're A Good Man, Charlie Brown* and played Glinda, the Good Witch of the North in the smash hit musical, *Wicked*. *Glee* was not the first time that she had shown of her prodigious vocal talent on TV before, either: she was one of the stars of the critically acclaimed *Pushing Daisies* (2007), now widely considered one of the best shows to be cancelled before its time. She even won a Primetime Emmy Award for Outstanding Supporting Actress in a Comedy in 2009 for her portrayal of Olive Snook. In one episode of *Pushing Daisies*, she sings 'Hopelessly Devoted to You' by Olivia Newton-John.

When the *Glee* cast found out that Kristin was to appear on the show, they were so excited. So many of the cast – especially those with prior experience on stage – looked up to her as one of the legends of the trade. Chris revealed to *E! Online*, 'They told us in a dance rehearsal that Kristin was going to be doing the show and I just sat there stiff. And I just stayed like that for five minutes. I think I peed a little. And then she was here and I wanted her so much to like me and fall in love with me.'

Her character, April Rhodes, is a former William McKinley High Glee Club member whose career in music – along with the rest of her life – falls by the wayside once she leaves high school. Will finds a loophole wherein because April never properly graduated from high school, she is eligible to come back and join the Glee Club. Kristin gets to sing 'Maybe This Time' from *Cabaret* in a duet with Lea Michele, 'Alone' by Heart with Matthew Morrison and Carrie Underwood's 'Last Name' with the entire New Directions ensemble.

And the cast had nothing but great things to say about her performance. 'Kristin Chenoweth will blow you away!' Jane Lynch predicted to *TV Guide* magazine. '[S]he knocks it out of the park. She blows the roof off the school. We were so lucky to have her, and she was a doll! A true professional, and lots of fun.'

Kevin McHale followed up Jane's comments, saying, 'I'm in awe of [Kristin]. She's absolutely brilliant. We get to watch her sing and it was like Jesus was right there! I'll never forget that – none of us will.'

Fortunately, there is scope to bring April Rhodes back on the scene, as everyone wants to work with Kristin again. 'I think with somebody like her, to be so talented, witty and charming in real life and behind the camera, and have so much respect from everybody on our set... a lot of them hadn't worked with her before, but she didn't have to demand respect, it was just [given to her] because she's such a kind and generous person and so easy to work with,' said Dianna Agron.

The critics liked her performance too. Kristin received the 2009 Satellite Award for Outstanding Guest Star.

Another big-name musician joined the cast with the introduction of the Jane Adams School for Girls. Their coach was the singer, Eve – who won a Grammy for her hit single 'Let Me Blow Ya Mind' and has a lot of experience in front of the camera. She was in the movie *Barbershop* and even had her own sitcom, aptly titled *Eve*. But Ryan Murphy's first choice was the powerhouse diva herself: Whitney Houston – who pulled out before filming began. Even Eve admits that would have been great to see: 'I would've loved to watch that myself,' she told *TV Guide*. 'I think it would've been different in a sense because she's an original diva. She would've brought a whole other energy, which would've been amazing.'

Like Josh Groban, Eve is an accomplished musician who wasn't asked to sing during her short time on *Glee*. Not that she didn't want to sing and she confirmed she would be back in a shot, if they wanted her: 'If I'm asked to do it, I definitely would. It's just a really well-made, smart show.'

That seems to be a common theme with guest stars. They want to come back again, as often as possible! Meanwhile, the stars are also lining up to be part of the last half of the season and Murphy seems spoiled for choice.

One of the first new guests to be announced was *Grease* star Olivia Newton-John. She had already had a song covered in *Glee* (by Kristin Chenoweth), but rumours of her appearance sent waves of excitement through the Gleek community. However, this probably had less to do with Ms Newton-John's cameo and more with the prospect of Jane Lynch singing on screen for the first time. The plan was for the two to duet to 'Physical'.

'I'm so excited, I can't see straight! [Olivia] provided the soundtrack for my tortured adolescence. Her charitable work and commitment to making others' lives and the life of the planet better is so inspiring,' Jane told *E! Online*. Ryan Murphy added, 'Olivia loves the show and is a great idol of mine.' Jane Lynch's Sue Sylvester is also set to get a new rival, in the form of *Saturday Night Live* actress Molly Shannon.

Many of the casts' idols were coming to *Glee*, but so far none of the *American Idols*. There were strong rumours that Adam Lambert, the flamboyant runner-up on *Idol* season 8, would join the show as a kind of mentor for Kurt. However, he denied the rumour on his official Twitter: 'Glee guest star rumor: it's a rumor. Sorry guys.'

GUEST STARS GALORE!

Another strong rumour buzzing around the *Glee* forums involved the other big Broadway star from *Wicked*: Idina Menzel. 'I know that she would love [to guest star on *Glee*],' said Taye Diggs, Menzel's husband, to *Fancast*. Many fans thought that Idina should play the role of Rachel Berry's biological mother, considering the striking resemblance between Idina and Lea Michele. 'We knew [the resemblance] existed far, far before the TV world did,' said Taye. In fact, Idina and Lea are big fans of each other's work and have seen each other on stage many times.

Although the role of Lea's mother was not to be, Idina signed up to join the cast as the coach of Vocal Adrenaline, the rival Glee Club to New Directions and the best show choir in Ohio. This is to be a recurring guest spot and like Kristin, Idina is bound to have a lasting impact on the cast.

Two other confirmed guests are *How I Met Your Mother* star Neil Patrick Harris and *Buffy the Vampire Slayer* creator Joss Whedon. Harris is to appear the episode that Joss Whedon is set to direct. This caused another big stir in the *Glee* world as both are really admired in the entertainment industry. The two had already worked together on a musical web series called *Dr. Horrible's Sing Along Blog* (2008). Neil first showed off his singing skills to the television world on the 100th episode of *How I Met Your Mother*, but he has also had experience on Broadway in shows such as *Sweeney Todd*, *Rent* and *Cabaret*, so he's no stranger to belting out tunes.

Joss Whedon is no stranger to directing musical television either. During the sixth season of *Buffy*, he directed an episode called 'Once More, With Feeling', which featured original music written by Whedon and is often considered the forerunner to *Glee*. Murphy had seen the episode and told *Entertainment Weekly*: 'Joss directed one of the great musical episodes in the history of television on *Buffy* so this is a great, if unexpected, fit. I'm thrilled he'll be loaning us his fantastic groundbreaking talent.'

Whedon's involvement is bound to draw new fans to the show, people who perhaps didn't give *Glee* a chance initially. Having Joss on board is like a signal that this is television worth watching and he has millions of cult followers. The *Philadelphia Daily News* explained it best, saying that Joss is 'an object of worship for viewers who like their television smart and funny and transcendent.'

There are myriad other rumours too, some stronger than others. Jennifer Lopez is a very strong rumour, with Ryan Murphy confirming at the Golden Globe Awards that he had a meeting lined up with her. But Murphy is careful. 'I don't want to stunt-cast too much,' he told *Entertainment Weekly*, 'because I think the [musical] numbers are already so extravagant. If I do Jennifer [Lopez], I would want her to be, like, a lunch lady. And

GUEST STARS GALORE!

Brad Falchuk is obsessed with having Bruce Springsteen on the show, so I'm sure we'll go after him at some point.' For a while, Julia Roberts looked likely to join the set too. It isn't so far fetched, especially considering Murphy has a habit of recruiting colleagues and Julia was working with him on the movie *Eat, Pray, Love* as the *Glee* episodes were airing for the first time in the US.

Even if celebrities don't get the chance to appear in the back nine episodes of the first season, there's still plenty of time! The permanent cast are excited by the possibilities and they all have their own ideas on who would make a great addition to the cast. Jenna Ushkowitz wants to see more Broadway stars come on board. She told *Teen Daily*: 'Going along with finding someone like Kristin who broke into film, broke into Broadway, and broke into television and kind of paved the way for people like Matthew Morrison, myself, and Lea Michele, somebody like that. Someone like Hugh Jackman I think would be great and he's sexy!'

Lea Michele wants to see Justin Timberlake in on the action. He was already referenced in Episode 2, 'Showmance', as someone able to combine performing with other pursuits such as fashion design and movies. 'Aside from being an incredible singer and dancer, he's also a fantastic comedic actor, and that is a great cocktail for being on *Glee*,' she told *E!* 'And I think he and Matt [Morrison] would have a fantastic dance-off.'

It looks as though this could become a reality: Justin expressed an interest to an *E!* red carpet correspondent but he said, 'No one's asked me to be on *Glee*.' Matthew Morrison, who has also been gunning to see him on the show, said, 'Okay, I'm on the phone. I'll get his number tonight.'

Dianna's choice is more offbeat: 'It might never happen, but I'm just gonna keep saying this: Christopher Walken. I think he would be amazing! He's so funny and I'm sure he can sing as well as he can dance.'

Even actors who haven't sung and danced in a public forum before are expressing an interest. Milla Jovovich, of *Resident Evil* fame, told *TV Guide*: 'I would go on it in a second! It would be a laugh to be in Sue's camp – I love her. It's a really inspiring show. I would have been on it without any other guest stars going on, I've been watching it since the day it came out.'

One thing's for certain, Murphy, Falchuk and Brennan will never bring a guest star onto the show just for star power. Whether it's comedic timing, singing prowess or smooth dance moves, they must add something.

'We've had a bunch of guest stars and they made the show so fantastic,' said Lea Michele. 'In my opinion, the show is like a ten and then you have these people come in and they make it like 100!'

EPISODE GUIDES

'PILOT: THE DIRECTOR'S CUT'

The first episode of *Glee* opens with the Cheerios. The high-school cheerleaders, all perfectly coiffed and flashing pearly-white grins, are performing an acrobatic routine under the watchful eye of head coach Sue Sylvester. Her biting opening line sets the tone for the whole show: 'You think this is hard? Try being waterboarded – *that's* hard!'

Cut to our first glimpse of teacher Will Schuester, who arrives at school in a beaten-up old car with an Ohio licence plate reading RP8 9624. In quick succession we are introduced to Finn Hudson and Noah 'Puck' Puckerman, with the rest of the football team, and Kurt Hummel, a well-dressed young student who is about to get thrown into the dumpster – although not before he removes his new Marc Jacobs jacket.

Will enters William McKinley High School – the main setting for the show. He stops at a trophy case and instantly we get a glimpse of his nostalgia as he spies the trophy for the 1993 show choir. A plaque underneath the image of the former Glee Club teacher reads: 'By its very definition, *Glee* is about opening yourself up to joy'.

GLEEFUL! MOMENT

The original pilot shown at screenings was an hour and a half long and had at least four additional scenes which were cut to bring viewing time down to fit in a one-hour television slot. The cut scenes were: a flashback to the original 1993 Glee Club Invitational, Will trying to make New Directions wear the hideous orange and yellow 1993 costumes, Puck auditioning for the Glee Club and an extended scene of Sandy Ryerson rehearsing.

Next we meet the current Glee Club teacher, Sandy Ryerson, who is playing the piano in accompaniment to a young male student, who is singing 'Where is Love?' from *Oliver!* Sandy gets a little too close to the student for comfort, caressing the boy's stomach while joining in the harmony of the duet. But someone is watching...

EPISODE 1.01: 'PILOT: THE DIRECTOR'S CUT'

In the teacher's lounge, we meet football coach Ken Tanaka and Emma Pillsbury, the redheaded guidance counsellor with an obvious crush on Will. Emma pulls out a pair of disposable gloves and reveals her obsessive compulsion for cleanliness. She also reveals that Sandy has been fired.

Will has only one question: 'Who will take over Glee Club?'

He takes this question straight to Principal Figgins' office, where he proposes that he should take on the mantle. He'll have to pay $60/month out of his own pocket for the privilege. Money is already tight in the Schuester household and Will doesn't know how he's going to break the news to Terri, his wife, but in the middle of the night, he has an epiphany: he is going to run Glee Club, and he's going to call it 'New Directions'.

He posts a New Directions sign-up sheet in the school hallway. Mercedes Jones is first to audition, belting out the Aretha Franklin classic 'Respect'. Following her is Kurt Hummel, obviously released from the dumpster. He chooses to sing 'Mr. Cellophane' from *Chicago* and wins over Will with his impressive falsetto. Next is Tina Cohen-Chang, an Asian girl with a Goth streak and a stutter (even when writing her name). She performs a raunchy rendition of 'I Kissed A Girl'.

Finally we meet Rachel Berry, the girl who turned

Sandy in – ostensibly for his inappropriate behaviour with a male student but really because he robbed her of her all-important solo. She sings 'On My Own' from the seminal Broadway classic, *Les Misérables*. We learn that she has two gay fathers, she's über-competitive and, tellingly, she thinks 'being anonymous is worse than being poor.'

After the auditions are over, the resulting Glee Club is... less than compelling. Even the Glee Club members themselves aren't very enthusiastic. It's Artie Abrams (a young man in a wheelchair, whose audition we don't get to see) who sings 'Sit Down, You're Rocking the Boat' with Rachel, and Rachel insists she needs a stronger leading man, who can keep up with her vocal talents. It looks as if New Beginnings might be over before it even gets a chance to start.

Will goes to Sheets-N-Things, where his frenetic wife is employed, to explain his ever-increasing workload. It's there that he bumps into Sandy and he finds out that he has been given a prescription for medical marijuana and is now selling it at a hefty profit.

There's only one way Glee Club is going to survive and that's if more kids sign up. Will makes a misguided decision to ask Sue Sylvester for help in recruiting within the Cheerios but she soon sets him straight: Glee kids are the lowest of the low on the high-school social ladder while the cheerleaders are right there at the top. Emma gives a disheartened Will a pep talk and he is once more inspired to try and find a few popular kids to join his singing troupe.

He convinces Coach Tanaka to let him talk to the football players. The meeting is a complete disaster, although it does lead to Will overhearing high-school quarterback Finn singing REO Speedwagon's 'I Can't Fight this Feeling Anymore' in the shower. He realises that this is why he wanted to start Glee Club all along – to help talented kids fulfil their potential even when they don't know they have it themselves. Not content to wait for Finn to sign up, Will blackmails him by planting some of Sandy's marijuana in his locker. In return for not handing him over to the authorities (or, more terrifyingly, not telling Finn's mum about the incident), Finn agrees to attend weekly Glee Club rehearsals.

It turns out that this might be just what Finn has wanted all along. A flashback reveals that when he was a young boy, he was influenced by one of his mother's ex-boyfriends: a lawn painter, who was a wannabe rocker. The ex-boyfriend and a young Finn sing 'Lovin' Touchin' Squeezin'' by Journey and for the first time, Finn discovers his love of music. When the boyfriend deserts Finn and his mum, Finn vows to do anything just to make his mum proud.

So Finn joins New Beginnings and his first song is a duet with Rachel: 'You're The One That I Want' from

Grease. With two charismatic leads on board, the Glee Club members can see their luck is about to change.

While things are finally going the right way at school, Will's home life is starting to fall apart. He is on the receiving end of some harsh criticism from Terri and they get into a massive row about spending. She spends too much at furniture stores like Pottery Barn and he, quite frankly, doesn't make enough to keep her in the manner that she would like. She pressures him to start making more money, suggesting he join an accountancy firm, and ridicules his nostalgic dreams of restarting a Glee Club.

Emma willingly accompanies Will on a Glee Club field trip to watch rival school Carmel High's Glee Club team Vocal Adrenaline, their biggest competition for the regional title. Meanwhile, Rachel subtly tries to feel out Finn's interest in her, but to no avail; he reveals that he already has a girlfriend – the perfect blonde cheerleader and president of the celibacy club, Quinn Fabray.

Once they're all seated in the audience, Will assures his team that Vocal Adrenaline have nothing on the McKinley High gang. The truth, however, is suddenly revealed as an incredibly polished, well-coached, high-energy Vocal Adrenaline team dazzle through a rendition of Amy Winehouse's 'Rehab'.

Quite appropriately, Tina stutters, 'We're doomed.'

And there's more bad news on the way for New

Directions, although it seems like good news for Will. Terri announces they're going to have a baby. Will is incredibly excited but this forces him to take stock of their financial situation. In the end, he decides to hand in his notice at the school and apply to become an accountant. For the first time, we get to hear Mr Schuester's voice as he picks up a guitar in an empty auditorium and sings 'Leaving on a Jet Plane'.

With Mr Schuester gone, Finn decides to quit Glee Club as well. He has had enough of the harassment from his football teammates and is ready to put music behind him. But a 'welcome back gift' from the football team in the form of an opportunity to bully the wheelchair-assisted Artie causes him to change his mind. He has the biggest epiphany of the episode: that they're all losers, just by virtue of living in Lima. If he has any chance of getting anywhere in the world, he's going to have to pursue both passions. So he's not going to give up Glee Club, but neither is he going to abandon football. Both teams need him, and he's not about to choose one over the other.

Meanwhile, New Directions is hardly the same without its head teacher and lead male vocal. Rachel is trying to take over the club but is coming up against a lot of resistance from Mercedes and Kurt. Finn shows up – much to the rest of Glee Club's surprise – and reunites the team by allowing everyone to bring their own special ability to the table.

Meanwhile, Emma is giving a pep talk of her own to Will. She shows him a video of the 1993 Glee team performing the disco hit 'That's The Way (I Like It)' at the national competition. It brings back great memories for Will, but he is unable to shake off the feeling that it's more important to start earning more money for his growing family.

GLEEFUL! MOMENT

What does Will mean when he tells Rachel to hit the 'ones and fives'?

Most music is written in 4/4 time, so beats one and five are the downbeats of the song.

A gloomy Will passes by the auditorium at the same time as his kids are belting out 'Don't Stop Believin''. Suddenly, seeing all the talent finally come together – along with the slightest hint that they might actually have the ability to win competitions – is just the impetus he needs. He's going to stay because as much as Glee Club needs him, he needs Glee even more.

EPISODE 1.01: 'PILOT: THE DIRECTOR'S CUT'

Episode 1.01: The Music

Opening Cheerleading Scene: 'Let Me Be', Josh Gabriel

Opening Credits: 'Shining Star', Earth, Wind & Fire

Sandy Ryerson and Student: 'Where is Love?', *Oliver!*

Background Music: 'Flight of the Bumblebee', Nikolai Rimsky-Korsakov (sung a capella by The Swingle Singers)

Background Music: 'Soul Bossa Nova', Quincy Jones (sung a capella by The Swingle Singers)

Mercedes' Audition: 'Respect', Aretha Franklin

Kurt's Audition: 'Mr. Cellophane', *Chicago*

Tina's Audition: 'I Kissed A Girl', Katy Perry

Rachel's Audition: 'On My Own', *Les Misérables*

Background Music: 'Golliwog's Cakewalk', Claude Debussy (sung a capella by The Swingle Sisters)

First Rehearsal: 'Sit Down, You're Rockin' the Boat', *Guys and Dolls*

Store Background Music: 'Raindrops Keep Fallin' on My Head', Burt Bacharach

Background Music: 'A Fifth of Beethoven', Walter Murphy (sung a capella by The Swingle Sisters and Shlomo)

Finn in the Shower: 'Can't Fight This Feeling', REO Speedwagon

Finn Flashback: 'Lovin' Touchin' Squeezin'', Journey

Finn's First Rehearsal: 'You're The One That I Want', *Grease*

Finn and Quinn: 'Chewing Gum' (Vocal Mix), *Annie*

Vocal Adrenaline Performance: 'Rehab', Amy
  Winehouse

Steel Drum Band: 'Don't Worry Be Happy', Bobby
  McFerrin

Background Music: 'Allegro (From Sonata No. 14 –
  Moonlight Sonata)', Ludwig van Beethoven (sung
  a capella in the background)

Finn's Dream and Final Performance: 'Don't Stop
  Believin'', Journey

1993 Glee Club song: 'That's the Way (I Like It)',
  KC and the Sunshine Band

Will and Emma: 'Looking Back', Kerry Muzzey.

GLEEFUL! MOMENT

The song played during the closing credits was written specially for the show by James S. Levine.

'SHOWMANCE'

The episode begins in the same way as the pilot, with Mr Schuester pulling into the parking lot – although this time, his licence plate reads 'GLEE'. Nothing much has changed – Will chats to various members of the Glee Club and waves to the football team – right before they toss Kurt back into the dumpster.

Emma orchestrates an 'accidental' bump into Will and he thanks her for convincing him to stay with Glee Club. They are interrupted by the Cheerios, who announce that Sue Sylvester has demanded a meeting with Will. He heads there straightaway.

Sue breaks down the main issue for Will: Glee Club doesn't have enough members to qualify for regionals and if they don't appear at the competition then the club will be cut from the school's budget. Will insists she has nothing to worry about. Glee will perform – and win.

Sue's not the only one trying to disband New Directions. Quinn and Finn are arguing in front of his locker – Quinn believes Finn is sacrificing their popularity for singing. She tries to bribe him to leave the club with an offer to touch her breast – over the bra, of course. Rachel overhears and hangs around by her locker but is relieved when Finn tells Quinn not to worry so much.

Quinn comes over to Rachel and warns her not to get too close to her man. Rachel comes up with a witty remark in reply but the effect is somewhat dampened when Puck throws a blue slushie in her face.

In the rehearsal studio, the Glee kids are practising 'Le Freak'. They don't seem to be 'getting' it and Will becomes frustrated with them. In turn, they complain that the song, with its seventies' cheesy dance moves, just isn't doing it for them. Will then breaks the even worse news: they have to perform the disco number in front of the whole school in an effort to recruit more members. 'I'm dead,' says Finn – no doubt voicing the feelings of the whole Glee Club.

Meanwhile, Terri has managed to convince Will that they need to buy a new house before their baby arrives. A flashback to a visit from Terri's sister, Kendra – complete with docile husband and screaming triplets – indicates that it was the sister who initially came up with the idea. She points out the inadequacy of their current home and casually brings up that they should look at brand new houses closer to them.

The new homes are gorgeous but of course, they're not being shown around the 'basic model' – this house has all the bells and whistles, including a grand foyer, sun nook, polished door handles and banisters made by Ecuadorian children. Terri falls instantly in love. Will almost faints after learning how much it's all going to cost.

GLEEFUL! MOMENT

Terri calls the decision to choose between a 'sun nook' or a 'grand foyer' her very own Sophie's Choice. The phrase 'Sophie's Choice' comes from the 1979 William Styron novel by the same name and refers to a tragic decision between two equally unbearable options. Clearly Terri is exaggerating.

But Will wants to do anything to make Terri's dream happen so he asks her for one compromise – sun nook or grand foyer – before agreeing to sign the papers.

At the same time, he makes more compromises with New Directions and brings a new song to rehearsal: Kanye's 'Gold Digger'. He tempers their enthusiasm by saying they don't have time to learn the song before the assembly. Finn backs off from attempting the solo, clearly intimidated by the thought of rapping and walking at the same time. Will shows him how it's done with a show-stopping rap that reveals his immense breadth of talent.

Meanwhile, in the bathroom Emma hears someone throwing up in one of the stalls. She goes over to investigate and finds Rachel bent over the toilet bowl. She hasn't actually been able to throw up yet – Emma reassures her that's a good thing – and they go back to Emma's office to have a talk.

Emma asks Rachel why she is attempting bulimia. Rachel says it's because she wants to be thin and pretty, and attract the attention of the guy she has a crush on. She asks Emma if she's ever had an intense crush. Emma adamantly denies it, but we know better as the scene cuts to her crying alone in her car to 'All By Myself'. Her solution – find something she has in common with her crush and things might develop naturally – seems to cheer Rachel up, however.

EPISODE 1.02: 'SHOWMANCE'

Has something happened already? The next scene sees Rachel and Finn in the Principal's office and the look on Sue's face suggests she's caught Rachel and Finn doing something totally disgusting and inappropriate together. But Will gets Rachel to tell the whole story and it turns out she and Finn used the Cheerios' photocopier to make recruitment posters for New Directions. Rachel's logic was if they made posters and got new people to join that way, they wouldn't have to embarrass themselves in front of the whole school. They get out of trouble by agreeing to pay for the copies but their reasoning still won't fly with Will – he insists on them performing 'Le Freak'.

After catching Principal Figgins cleaning up Sue's congealed protein shake from the office floor, Will also gets the opportunity to take on a night-time shift as the school janitor. He needs to make more money to afford his new house and so even taking the job on half-salary is worth it to him.

Rachel tries to get closer to Finn by joining the celibacy club. She's disappointed to learn that they separate the boys and girls for the first half of the club meeting, and so she's stuck listening to Club President Quinn going on about the Cheerios' motto: 'It's all about the teasing, not about the pleasing'.

Meanwhile, in the boys' meeting, they discuss the issue of 'arriving too soon' when they're with a girl. Finn claims he doesn't have a problem, but a flashback shows differently. In fact, the only thing he can do to prevent the issue is to think back to the time when he crashed into a postman while learning to drive.

When the boys and girls finally get together, they practise the 'immaculate affection', which is when couples attempt to hug each other separated by a balloon. If the balloon bursts, the hug is in violation of the Celibacy Club code. Finn's pops – oops – and Rachel protests the Club's message. She claims that high-school kids need sex, that it's unnatural for them to try and abstain and that they should instead focus on being educated and protected. She also lets out a big revelation: girls want sex as much as boys. This doesn't go down well with Quinn but it does give Rachel an idea: she decides that the Glee Club needs to sex it up to win over the high-school student body.

Will is doing his first shift as a janitor but is caught by Emma: she agrees to keep his extra job a secret between them and even stays to help out. Will manages to figure out why Emma is so afraid of germs. She explains that as a little girl she was taken to a dairy farm where her brother pushed her into a runoff lagoon – a pond where the manure and other waste products is gathered before being treated – and she's never recovered from the experience.

The day of the dreaded assembly dawns, but there's a surprise in store for Will as Rachel has changed the music without telling him. Instead of disco, it's Salt-n-Pepa's 'Push It' with naughty lyrics and raunchy dance moves, including a lot of simulated sex. By the end, it's clear they've accomplished their goal of winning over the students – the whole auditorium erupts into applause.

They haven't done so well in winning over Will, however – nor Sue or the parents who call the school to complain. Principal Figgins won't agree to Sue's suggestion of disbanding the club, though: instead he gives Will a list of songs pre-approved from his pastor. He even allows New Directions a larger budget to buy more costumes.

Ken and Emma's relationship amps up a notch after he gives a straight-talking speech about how he's prepared to take care of her and 'put up with her crazy'. She finally gives in and agrees to go on a date with him to Tulipalooza.

GLEEFUL! MOMENT

When Finn flashes back to the moment he hits the postman, the car has no rear-view mirror. The attachment for it is there on the windscreen (windshield), but no actual mirror.

While Rachel and Finn rehearse in the auditorium, they take a break and start chatting. Chatting leads to kissing, but Finn quickly bolts just as things get hot. Meanwhile, Quinn shows up in Will's office to audition for Glee Club. Afterwards, Sue decides to have Quinn, Brittany and Santana Lopez be her spies within Glee.

Terri goes to the doctor's only to discover that she isn't actually pregnant. Instead, she's having a 'hysterical pregnancy' – her body is simulating the effects of being pregnant because she wants it so much. When Will arrives home, she can't bring herself to tell him the truth. Instead, she tells him that she doesn't need a big new house after all and so wants him to quit his night-time janitorial shifts. She also digs the deceit deeper by telling him they're having a baby boy.

Although Glee Club can't succeed without additional members, Rachel soon finds out one of the downsides of having the Cheerios join New Directions: no more solo. Also, despite the kiss it looks like Finn isn't prepared to give up Quinn for Rachel in any hurry, and Rachel pours out her heart and soul in 'Take A Bow'.

Episode 1.02: The Music

Background music: 'Ain't That a Kick in the Head',
  Dean Martin

Rehearsal song: 'Le Freak', Chic

Will's rap: 'Gold Digger', Kanye West featuring
  Jamie Foxx

Assembly song: 'Push It', Salt-n-Pepa

Emma crying in her car: 'All By Myself', Eric Carmen

Cheerio's audition: 'Say a Little Prayer', Dionne
  Warwick

Rachel's song: 'Take A Bow', Rihanna.

GLEEFUL! MOMENT

The brochures that Emma Pillsbury keeps in her office are titled: 'Ouch! That Stings!', 'Divorce: Why Your Parents Stopped Loving You', 'I Can't Stop Touching Myself', 'Radon: The Silent Killer', 'My Mom's Bipolar and She Won't Stop Yelling', 'Wow! There's a Hair Down There' and 'So You Like Throwing Up: Understanding and Overcoming Bulimia'.

'ACAFELLAS'

We're introduced to Will's parents as they're having dinner with Will and Terri – Terri has made hamburger casserole. Will makes the big announcement that they're having a boy. Terri looks terrified, but she plays along with it and takes Will's mum to the craft room that she's going to turn into the baby's bedroom.

Alone with his dad, Will confesses his insecurities. His father blames himself – he believes that he set a bad example by not having the confidence to go for his dream of becoming a lawyer, instead settling for a job in insurance. He doesn't want Will to follow in his footsteps: he tells him he has six months to figure out if he has any guts.

New Directions is rehearsing a number with the three cheerleaders as their new members. They all seem less than impressed with Will's choreography – it's like 'Le Freak' all over again. Finally, Rachel speaks up – although we learn through flashbacks that she is being coached by the Cheerios – and says that the team needs to hire Dakota Stanley, who coaches Vocal Adrenaline.

This really eats away at Will's ebbing confidence and he vents his frustration to Emma. Emma assures him that it's okay for them to talk because they're both in a relationship – she's just started to date Ken Tanaka.

Sandy is back and we also meet the wood shop teacher, Henri, who has bandaged hands. It turns out he has an addiction to cough medicine and chopped off his thumbs while 'under the influence'. Howard, Terri's shop assistant from Sheets-N-Things, brings in a cake supposedly for celebrating Henri's return. Ironically, it reads 'Two Thumbs Up!' Will comments on how he enjoys hanging out with the guys and they each share a sob story, although none is more tragic than Henri's. To make him feel better, they start to sing 'For He's a Jolly Good Fellow'. Their smooth harmonies spark inspiration in Will: they should start an a cappella boy band.

GLEEFUL! MOMENT

The other names suggested for the boy band are 'Crescendudes' and 'Testostertones'.

EPISODE 1.03: 'ACAFELLAS'

Howard provides the name, Acafellas, and they begin rehearsals without Sandy – who is deemed creepy. Will thinks one perk of being in a boy band is his wife's renewed interest in making love... although that may have more to do with her desperate need to get pregnant rather than his singing skills, smooth as they are!

Because Acafellas is his new passion, and still smarting from Rachel's dig at his choreography skills (he *is* sensitive), Will has more or less abandoned Glee Club. Rachel tries to apologise with cookies but Will still doesn't come back. Finn points out to Rachel that it was her fault, but she doesn't want to hear about it – at least, not from him. He then asks if Rachel ignoring him has something to do with their kiss in the auditorium. Rachel doesn't want to talk about it but has the last word – there are real feelings between them, Finn just doesn't have the guts to admit it.

Meanwhile, Sue is really impressed by her Cheerios' achievements so far when it comes to undermining the Glee Club. Everything seems to be falling apart at the seams, just as she wants it. She won't rest until New Directions is a thing of the past and the Cheerios can have their money back.

Mercedes is pining for a boyfriend. She asks Kurt if he's ever been kissed and he says no, but it's because they're both in Glee Club and so no one pays them any attention. The Cheerios take advantage of this perceived weakness in

Mercedes and see a chance to create more tension in the team. They convince her that going after Kurt is a good idea… and surprisingly, Mercedes warms to the idea.

It's the first Acafellas performance, which takes place in a local sports bar. They perform 'Poison' and in the crowd are Emma and Terri. It's also the first time that Terri gets a hint of Emma's feelings for her husband. The Acafellas are a hit, however, and sell out all their CDs. Principal Figgins loves the show too and asks them to perform for the PTA meeting to take the parents' minds off some of the problems at McKinley High.

The critics love the band too – they get a great review in the paper. But rejected Sandy storms in, demanding to be reinstated. He offers up an incentive: if he gets a spot in Acafellas, he'll get Josh Groban to come to the PTA meeting – and if they impress Josh Groban enough, they may get to be the opening act for his tour.

New Directions are driven to Carmel High in Kurt's very expensive Lincoln Navigator, which his father got him for his sweet sixteen. They are at Carmel to meet Dakota Stanley and convince him to choreograph for McKinley High. Two Vocal Adrenaline members are outside – one is throwing up in a rubbish bin – and they try to warn New Directions that it's not a good idea.

They're not going to be put off so easily, though, and they go inside to watch a Vocal Adrenaline number – another blatant reminder that they're nowhere near ready to compete at that level. They catch up with Dakota Stanley and he tells them his staggering fee: $8,000.

Quitting season is upon us. Both Howard and Henri are unable to continue in Acafellas and Finn quits the Glee Club because although he loves singing, he really can't take the taunting from his football team. Finn's departure gives Will an idea, however: he asks Finn to fill one of the spots in Acafellas that has just opened up.

In a surprising turn of events, Puck decides he wants to join Acafellas too, although his motives are beyond questionable. He sees it as a way to meet older women while his pool cleaning business is on hold. His ideal woman is a MILF and this is the perfect way to meet her. Tanaka agrees to let him join their group, but makes him promise not to screw up. Will teaches the boys to dance by relating the hip movement to baseball.

It's the ultimate cliché – cheerleaders in skimpy bikinis at a car wash – but the Glee Club has to somehow raise funds if they want to hire Dakota Stanley. Kurt and Mercedes are washing Kurt's Navigator and Mercedes asks if they can make it official that they're a couple. Kurt tries to let her down gently by saying he's in love with someone else and Mercedes mistakenly thinks he means Rachel. Kurt doesn't deny it and Mercedes throws a rock through his windscreen, prompting her to launch into the amazing fantasy sequence 'Bust Ya Windows'.

Somehow they've made the money and Dakota is

conducting his first rehearsal. He doesn't last very long, however – after insulting everyone in the Glee Club except the Cheerios, Rachel stands up for the underdogs and fires him.

It's the big night for Acafellas – the PTA meeting. Ken is even putting on make-up for the event. It also turns out that Sandy has kept up his end of the bargain as Josh Groban is in the audience. Their performance is electric and they finish high on adrenaline.

But Josh Groban brings them down a notch when they find out that he only turned up to their show to file a restraining order against Sandy. Never mind, they get a touch of praise from him too but it's lost all of its meaning now they realise Acafellas won't go any bigger than a high-school stage. Will's okay with it – all he really wants to do is teach, anyway.

Sensing the competition from Emma, Terri hones in on Will and acts the supportive wife. In the meantime, Josh Groban starts hitting on Will's mum and Will's dad confesses that he's going to law school after all, inspired by his son.

Mercedes goes up to Kurt and apologises for breaking his car window. He forgives her and she tells him that she hopes it works out for him and Rachel. Kurt decides to come clean – and to come out of the closest. He admits that he's gay, and Mercedes convinces him that it's nothing to be ashamed about.

Everyone is happy... everyone, of course, except Sue. She can't believe how her plan has backfired so quickly.

And we even get a sense that the Cheerios are beginning to turn away from Sue's conniving ways and towards the Glee Club. Sue's going to have to act quickly if she wants to bring down New Directions.

Episode 1.03: The Music
Teachers' Lounge: 'For He's a Jolly Good Fellow'
Acafellas rehearsal: 'This Is How We Do It', Montell Jordan
Acafellas: 'Poison', Bell Biv DeVoe
Vocal Adrenaline: 'Mercy', Duffy
Mercedes Jones: 'Bust Ya Windows', Jazmine Sullivan
Puck: 'La Camisa Negra', Juanes
Acafellas: 'I Wanna Sex You Up', Color Me Badd

GLEEFUL! MOMENT

When Will opens the door to his apartment to find Sandy there, Sandy says: 'I'm ready for my close-up, Mr. DeMille!'

'Mr. DeMille' is the famous director Cecil B. DeMille and the line is from the 1950 movie, Sunset Boulevard. The quote is actually, 'Alright, Mr. DeMille, I'm ready for my close-up!' and was delivered by Norma Desmond, a one-time movie star, who is lost in the fantasy that she's in one of DeMille's movies.

EPISODE 1.04
'PREGGERS'

The episode opens inside Kurt's basement, where he – along with Tina and Brittany – is videotaping a rendition of Beyoncé's 'Single Ladies' while wearing a black unitard. They're interrupted by Kurt's dad, who looks very confused and wants to know what's going on: Kurt makes up a quick lie that he's wearing the unitard to work out, while Brittany makes things worse by saying he's been put on the football team as a kicker. Kurt's dad is suddenly proud of him and asks to be taken to the next game. Oops!

Meanwhile, Will and Terri's sister, Kendra, are helping Terri practise for the birth. Kendra has nothing but bad things to say about the process of giving birth and tries to persuade Will to be tough. Terri is extremely nervous about Will accidentally touching her stomach so she sends him out of the room. She confesses the fake pregnancy to her sister, who immediately comes up with a plan – they're going to find her a baby from somewhere and keep up the deception.

Back at school Emma tells Will and Ken that she spotted Sue Sylvester on the local news programme the previous night. Sue's been given her own segment to spout her special brand of Sue-wisdom, which she ends with: 'And that's how Sue C's it', holding up her hand in the shape of the letter 'C'. Sue turns up in the teachers' lounge and lauds her newfound local fame over the three.

Rachel is devastated in Glee Club rehearsal when Will gives the solo from *West Side Story* to Tina. She storms out of the rehearsal, something that has less and less of an impact every time she does it. Kurt corners Finn for a favour – a tryout for the football team so that he can keep up the ruse for his dad. Coach Ken is willing to give him a shot, mostly because his football team is so pathetic they've missed every conversion in the past twelve games. Kurt, of course, can't 'audition' for the position without warming up to 'Single Ladies' – which causes sniggers from the football team. But they aren't laughing when he kicks the ball straight through the goalposts: he's on the team.

Meanwhile, Sue is signing headshots at the local TV news station. The station manager, Mr. McClung, comes up to her and tells her that in order to keep her slot, she needs to make sure her Cheerios win nationals. Rumours have circulated that Glee Club is stealing all of Sue's talent. Now she's more determined than ever to bring down New Directions.

Then comes the big news of the episode: Quinn reveals to Finn that she's pregnant. They've never had sex so Quinn tells him that it's the result of an incident in a hot tub. Quinn is going to keep the baby but they are both devastated by the implications.

GLEEFUL! MOMENT

At the end of Principal Figgins' TV commercial for Mumbai Airlines, the voiceover says in Hindi: 'And keep in mind, Mumbai Airlines never crashes. Well, it crashes only a little.'

Sue pays a visit to the depressed Sandy, whose attempt at keeping a happy face crumbles at the first question: Sue offers him a way out of his misery – a position as the school's arts administrator so that he can finally wrench control of Glee Club away from Will. It turns out that Sue is blackmailing Principal Figgins with an old in-flight video that he once did for Mumbai Airlines in order to get her way. Rachel is key to bringing down Glee Club as she is the most talented of them all.

Together, they come up with a plan to steal her away: they're going to give her the lead in the musical *Cabaret*. Just as predicted, Rachel auditions for the show and gets the part.

Will, however, sees right through Sue's plan and tries to convince Rachel it's not the right thing to do. But Rachel is still mad at Mr. Schuester for taking away her solo and she's not going to give up the lead role. As if to prove a point, Tina sings 'Tonight' from *West Side Story* and doesn't quite hit the last note. Tina wants Mr. Schuester to give the solo back to Rachel, but Will thinks it's too late.

Finn shows up at the auditorium and bursts into tears in front of Will, then confesses Quinn's pregnancy. He doesn't want to be a 'Lima loser' – stuck in their small town for the rest of his life – he has bigger dreams, dreams that at least include going to college. But the only way he's going to get there is with a football scholarship and so he tells Will about his idea: he wants him to teach the team how to dance in the hope that it might loosen them up enough to start winning – in return, Will can try to recruit some male singers for New Directions.

As they're getting ready to go to bed, Will chats to Terri about Finn's dilemma and Quinn's pregnancy, and his wife realises she may be able to get her baby after all.

Finn was right and Coach Tanaka is willing to try

anything to invigorate his losing side. Will and Kurt teach the team the 'Single Ladies' dance. Afterwards, Finn tells his best friend Puck about Quinn's pregnancy. Puck then confronts Quinn and she reveals that although Puck is the real father, she doesn't want her baby raised by a 'Lima loser'. In tears, she runs to her car only to find Terri sitting in the passenger seat. Although Quinn is freaked out, Terri manages to convince her to take some pre-natal vitamins and sets herself up as a confidante.

Finally, it's time for the team's first game since the dance lessons – except the team is absolutely against doing the dance for fear of looking gay. Kurt's dad is in the stands, as are Will and Emma.

Of course, the McKinley High team are losing and with only one second to go, Finn calls a time out. He convinces the team to do the dance. The music begins blasting over the speakers and the whole football team starts 'Single Ladies', completely throwing the other side offguard, and they end up scoring a touchdown to tie the game. Now it's Kurt's time to shine. He does his warm up and kicks the point. The team wins! Kurt's dad goes wild with excitement. Finn and Quinn kiss, leaving Puck feeling disappointed.

Back home, Kurt's dad tells him how proud he is of him. Kurt realises this is the perfect moment to tell his dad his big 'secret' – that he is gay. His father confesses to knowing already and tells him that he's going to support and love his son, no matter what.

Finn finally seems ready to embrace fatherhood as he offers Quinn his old baby blanket, which is his only memory of his own father. Puck comes up to them both and starts insulting Quinn, which aggravates him and so Puck backs down, although he's clearly still frustrated by Quinn's rejection.

At Glee Club, Rachel thinks Will has come to his senses and is going to offer her the 'Maria' solo – except he still gives it to Tina. It's the last straw for Rachel, who quits the club to work exclusively on *Cabaret* for Sandy. Sue's corner ends the show with an ominous tone – she might be down, but she's not out.

Episode 1.04: The Music
Kurt's basement: 'Single Ladies (Put A Ring On It)',
  Beyoncé
Rachel's audition: 'Taking Chances', Celine Dion
Tina in the auditorium: 'Tonight', *West Side Story*
Background music: 'The Star-Spangled Banner',
  Francis Scott Key.

'THE RHODES NOT TAKEN'

New Directions are practising 'Don't Stop Believin'' again (how do you think they might feel if they realised their hit had gone to No. 2 in the UK singles chart?), but this time Quinn has the lead female role. Unfortunately, she can't sing for very long because she keeps getting morning sickness. The Glee Club actually lament the loss of Rachel – even though they found her annoying, she was their best singer. Mr Schuester tells them they have to forget about Rachel and focus on doing their best anyway.

Quinn's morning sickness woes cause Will to contemplate Terri's lack of pregnancy-related issues. He asks her about it over dinner at a local restaurant. Terri quickly covers by claiming that all her sickness takes place at work. Will suddenly recognises their waiter as one of his former students who has transferred to Carmel High to perform in Vocal Adrenaline. He reveals to Will that he has had to repeat his senior year six times in order to stay on. That gives Will an idea.

Finn is in Emma's office: she has brought him in for counselling – she's not supposed to know about Quinn's pregnancy but Will has obviously told her all about it. Rather than a football scholarship, her solution is that Finn should try and get a music scholarship through Glee Club. The only way this can happen is if Rachel rejoins the team – that way, they might have a shot at nationals.

Rachel is interviewed by Jacob Ben Israel, a reporter for their school newspaper. He tries to get her to show him her bra in exchange for a good review. Rachel refuses in disgust.

GLEEFUL! MOMENT

Equus, the play that Sandy claims he's going to produce next, features full-frontal male nudity. Harry Potter star Daniel Radcliffe appeared as Alan Strang in a revival at the Gielgud Theatre in London's West End.

Finn decides that the best way to get Rachel to join Glee Club again is to seduce her back into it. He offers to help her rehearse her lines – somewhere private, of course.

Back in Emma's office, Emma reluctantly gives Will the file on an ex-student named April Rhodes. April was once the star of the McKinley High Glee Club and was Will's first crush in high school – before his wife Terri, of course. Emma warns him of the dangers of digging up the past but he isn't worried. He gets into contact with April immediately and drives over to meet her.

It looks like April has done well for herself. She lives in a massive mansion and offers Will a glass of wine. It's only when a real estate agent shows up with some prospective buyers that Will realises April is only squatting. In reality, her life after high school has become a mess. She was never able to make it to New York to live out her dream, became an alcoholic and didn't even graduate. But this is where Will senses an opportunity. He offers to enrol her in his Spanish class so she can get the extra credit to graduate. In return, he has a new leading lady for his Glee Club.

At first, New Directions are sceptical. April is clearly a mature student and they can't see how she can compare to Rachel. That is until April begins to sing – and we see Rachel singing the same song for Stanley in the auditorium. It's the battle of the divas. April very obviously proves to the Glee Club that she can more than lead them into the finals – she could carry them on one massive high note.

There's still work to do, so Will asks April to make

sure she plays nicely with the kids. April manages to find the sleaziest ways possible to ingratiate herself into the team: she gives Kurt some alcohol and male porn, teaches Tina and Mercedes how to shoplift and accompanies the football team into their shower. That's one way to make friends.

Meanwhile, Rachel struggles under Sandy's direction for *Cabaret*. He's getting equally frustrated and almost takes the role away from her. Rachel then takes up Finn's offer of rehearsing her lines. He tries to get her to come back to Glee. She's still not sure so he offers to take her bowling to loosen up a bit. Rachel then realises Will has replaced her with April as he kicks her out for the rehearsal space.

GLEEFUL! MOMENT

After Kurt throws up on her, Emma says she got 'the full Silkwood' from the hospital. Silkwood refers to the 1983 Oscar-nominated film about the true story of Karen Silkwood (Meryl Streep), who takes multiple chemical showers when she becomes contaminated by radiation while investigating wrongdoings at a plutonium plant.

Kurt is blind drunk. Emma stops him to ask what's wrong and he throws up all over her shoes. For a germaphobe, this is the worst possible outcome. After her decontamination showers at the hospital, she tells Will that he's got to keep a closer eye on April – and on his own motives. She doesn't believe he has Glee Club's best intentions at heart at the moment.

Rachel breaks down in rehearsal for *Cabaret* and ends up crying in the bathroom. April comes in and makes her feel even worse by saying that she's not going to let go of her position as top singer in the school.

Rachel and Finn are on their bowling date and Finn smoothly corrects her technique. In a weird coincidence, April and Will are also bowling together. Will voices his concerns about April's attitude – and her sobriety – and she vows to behave better in the future. Then Will confesses his one regret: never singing with her in high school – she was his inspiration. But April's ready to remedy this right away and pulls him up onto a karaoke stage, where they sing a duet. In the meantime, Finn is still trying to persuade Rachel to return to Glee. Finn's bowling lessons obviously pay off as Rachel scores a strike. This leads to them kissing again and Rachel says she'll come back.

The other members of New Directions sense that something is up with Quinn. After a bit of speculation, Puck sets the record half-straight by telling them all that Quinn's pregnant with Finn's baby. Rachel makes her dramatic return to Glee Club but there's no welcome back banner – and when she hears about Quinn's pregnancy, she believes Finn has played her. She finds him and confronts him right away – straight after slapping him in the face. He admits that he needs her in Glee so that he can get a music scholarship but he swears the kiss was real. She doesn't want to hear any of it, however, and she doesn't want any part of Glee Club. Rachel goes to Sue and asks to be restored in her role in *Cabaret*, a request Sue is happy to bestow – along with full artistic control, Rachel's dream comes true.

New Directions are about to perform in their first invitational, except that their leading lady is completely plastered – obviously the plan to get back on the wagon fell by the wayside. Emma tries to convince Will that it's not a good idea to have April perform as it sets a bad example for the kids but he allows her to do so anyway. Rachel watches their performance and is clearly devastated that she's not up there with them.

Will comes to his senses and kicks April out of Glee. But she goes willingly. She realises that she's had her time in the limelight and wants someone else to have a chance to shine. Of course, that someone else is Rachel. With New Directions now properly together, they sing an amazing rendition of 'Somebody to Love' by Queen.

EPISODE 1.05: 'THE RHODES NOT TAKEN'

Episode 1.05: The Music

Rehearsals: 'Don't Stop Believin'', Journey

Background music: 'Heart of Glass', Blondie

April and Rachel dual: 'Maybe This Time', *Cabaret*

Background music: 'You Make My Dreams Come True',
  Hall & Oates

Rachel: 'Cabaret', *Cabaret*

Bowling Alley: 'I Want a New Drug', Huey Lewis

April and Will: 'Alone', Heart

April and New Directions: 'Last Name', Carrie
  Underwood

New Directions: 'Somebody to Love', Queen.

EPISODE 1.06
'VITAMIN D'

Once again, New Directions looks to be uninspired – what is it with these kids? This time, however, it's because they're feeling too confident: they've found out that their competition for sectionals is to be a deaf choir and an all-girls' reform school. What do they have to worry about?

Once again, Will vents to Emma about his worries. They flirt a little over mustard on Will's chin. Sue interrupts and explains her methods for creating a championship-level team to Will. Although Sue is obviously way meaner than Will could ever be, she does give him an idea... which is to inspire a little more competitiveness within the Glee team.

He divides the Glee Club into boys versus girls – and

of course, Kurt moves to join the girls' team although Will puts him back with the boys. He challenges them to create a mash-up of two songs that wouldn't normally go together. The winner gets to choose one of the songs for sectionals. It's a great prize and the girls seem to think they have it in the bag. It doesn't help that Finn looks as if he's about to fall asleep at any moment.

Meanwhile, Sue confides in her personal journal. She has spotted a tiny quiver in Quinn's cheerleading performance, which leads her to believe they're going to lose at nationals. As we already know, Sue is desperate to retain the crown. Quinn's excuse is that she's tired, but Sue knows the real reason – Glee Club. And her newest plan is more devilishly evil than before: if she can't destroy Will's Glee Club, she can at least set out to ruin his personal life.

Sue goes straight to the centre of the ticking time bomb and makes Terri aware of the goings-on between Will and Emma. Terri is sceptical, but increasingly nervous of losing Will, she agrees to come and work as the school nurse to check the situation out for herself. The position is vacant, but only because Sue tripped the former nurse down the stairs. Terri manages to convince Principal Figgins that she's the one for the job despite her apparent inexperience.

Will is in the teachers' lounge and is about to ask Emma to be the Glee Club's 'celebrity judge' in the boys versus girls' competition. Cue the entrance of Terri Schuester, who immediately comes and sits between the two of them. Taking advantage of Emma's mysophobia, Terri licks her finger and rubs lipstick off Emma's cup, which means Emma can no longer use it. Will expresses his disbelief at Terri's new position, but there's nothing he can do about it. At this point, he can't even pretend to be happy!

Finn's sleepiness is catching up to him in football practice. With everything he has going on, from Quinn to Rachel to football to the sheer effort of being popular, he can't concentrate on anything at all. Puck offers a solution he has used many times: go and see the school nurse, feign illness and nap for a few hours... except the new nurse has different plans.

Terri realises that Finn is the father of Quinn's baby (or so everyone believes) and she begins to interrogate him about his background. She then shares with him the remedy that enabled her to stay popular in her own high-school days: a little 'Vitamin D' for decongestant. It works a treat and Finn is buzzing. He gets all the guys to take a couple before their performance.

As a result of the Vitamin D inspiration, the boys' side knock it out of the park. The girls – who were just going to wing it – are unable to believe their eyes and ears. Will is also amazed but no one suspects anything fishy about their incredible energy levels.

Rachel and Quinn share a moment where Rachel

makes it clear to her that she has friends in Glee Club who will support her, no matter what. As her pregnancy develops and she becomes more of an outcast, Quinn's going to need all the support she can get.

Ken is in Terri's office to commiserate with her about their partners' flirting. Terri wants to get out of the job – she hates working a full week – and Ken reveals he has never had sex with Emma. Terri persuades him that the only solution is for him to propose to Emma and prescribes a little Vitamin D as a boost.

Kurt reveals the Vitamin D secret to the girls, who can't believe the boys cheated. Rachel confronts Finn in the hallway and reveals her intensive conditioning routine that helps keep her in top competitive shape – except the easy answer to their problems is to take Vitamin D as well. The girls' side pay a visit to Terri, who is happy to supply them.

Finally, Will can't take it any more and claims that he can't work and live with Terri at the same time. Terri is hurt and spots Emma watching them. She then spurs Ken on propose, which he does – much to Emma's horror.

It's now the girls' turn. Their mash-up is also fabulous and Will still doesn't realise anything is amiss despite Rachel's speaking rhythm speeding up to Formula-1 level. He also takes the opportunity to ask Emma about her decision regarding Ken's proposal. Emma still isn't sure.

EPISODE 1.06: 'VITAMIN D'

Terri wants to help make that decision for her. She confronts Emma, but Emma holds her own. Still, it's Terri who gets the last word and she convinces Emma to go for a man who is, at the very least, available.

Terri is now on a roll as she also gets a decision from Quinn: she's going to let her have the baby. Terri draws the line at paying for maternity clothes, which is a bit mean considering she's essentially going to take the baby 'under the table'.

Emma goes to Ken to clarify the definition of their marriage, which doesn't really sound much like a marriage at all. In fact, she wants to keep the whole thing a complete secret. But it's good enough for Ken and the two are engaged. Will finds out Emma has accepted Ken's proposal and he looks incredibly disappointed.

Finn calls Rachel out as a hypocrite for taking the drugs and they come clean to Will. Now the cat is well and truly out of the bag as Howard has been arrested for buying all the decongestant tablets for Terri on suspicion of running a meth lab. Will is upset with Terri, who resigns as school nurse, but Principal Figgins is angry with Will and says that he's too focused on the competitive aspect of Glee to make good decisions. In an ironic attempt to make things better, he orders Sue, the most competitive coach alive, to come on board as the co-chair. Of course, she's thrilled – now she can bring the club down from the inside.

Episode 1.06: The Music

Rachel's iPod alarm: 'Break My Stride', Matthew Wilder

Boys' mash-up: 'It's My Life', Bon Jovi and 'Confessions Part II', Usher

Girls' mash-up: 'Halo', Beyoncé and 'Walking On Sunshine', Katrina & The Waves.

GLEEFUL! MOMENT

Iqbal Theba plays Principal Figgins. He explained his character to *Starry Constellation* magazine: 'Figgins is somebody who wanted to be a CEO, but is not for some reason, whatever it may be. He wanted to be rich but now he has to live with the fact that he is a principal at a small town high school. It kind of shows on his body and the language he uses and the way he acts. I thought he's a guy who wanted to be somebody big, but he's not and now he has to deal with it.'

EPISODE 1.07

'THROWDOWN'

S ue and Will are in the middle of a slow motion, full-on screaming match. Sue's appointment as Glee Club co-captain has torn the New Directions apart. Although they pretend to be nice to each other in front of Principal Figgins, flashbacks show both Will and Sue are playing dirty. Will tries to get the kids on side by listening to their ideas while Sue needles right into the heart of the issue – the minority students don't feel their voices are being heard – and unveils a plan to bring New Directions down by dividing up the team.

Quinn and Finn are in the obstetrician's office and Quinn is having an ultrasound. They find out that the baby is a girl. Having driven the two teens to the doctor's, Will wonders why he's not more involved in his own wife's pregnancy.

Josh, the school gossip hound, tells Rachel that he's about to write a blog revealing Quinn's pregnancy. She begs him not to, promising to do anything he wants.

Sue's first order of business is to create an 'elite' Glee Club within New Directions called 'Sue's Kids'. Will protests, saying that it's against the rules, but ever prepared, Sue whips out the relevant paragraph in the rulebook and shuts him up. But she surprises Will by not picking her precious Cheerios but selecting all the visible minorities over to her side.

Will brings his frustration home and over dinner, confronts Terri about his lack of involvement in the pregnancy. She is mostly interested in finding out about Quinn's baby and her mind ticks over the possibilities as she realises her 'boy' needs to become a girl fast. Will insists on going to the next doctor's appointment with her.

Rachel reveals to Finn that she 'paid' Josh off to stop him from running the story. It turns out she had to give Josh a pair of her panties, but the ones she has given him aren't good enough – they still have the store tags on – so he asks for another pair or he'll blog the pregnancy.

'Sue's Kids' meet in the music room and are unsure what to expect. But Sue has pulled out all the stops and offers them up an awesome R&B song, 'Hate On Me', that allows everyone to shine. Will can't believe Sue has actually managed to win the kids over. This is especially infuriating as she puts up roadblocks in front of him at every turn –

even burning his sheet music! She says the reason why she's so against him is because she can't trust a man with curly hair and reveals her ultimate goal: to have Will fired.

Will resolves to get his own back. Encouraged by Terri –the ultimate schemer – he flunks all the Cheerios from his Spanish class so they're no longer academically eligible to be on the cheerleading squad. Sue is livid. Principal Figgins has had enough of Sue, however, and says Will is right. After Will leaves, Figgins reveals that Sue can no longer blackmail him with the in-flight video – he has already made it public and nobody cares. She goes on a rampage through the school.

During a Spanish test, Finn passes Quinn a note. He suggests the name 'Drizzle' for their baby. Quinn can't believe Finn's insensitivity – not only has he come up with a stupid name but also she's not planning on keeping the child and so she doesn't want to have to think of baby names at all. She asks him to not have an opinion and he asks her to be more like Rachel. Quinn reminds Finn that Rachel's only helping them out because she has a crush on him.

Puck is playing 'Ride Wit Me' on his guitar while the rest of the Glee Club has an impromptu jam session in the music room. They much prefer being together rather than separated into different groups but they're worried about the consequences, if Sue finds out.

Will gives the group his music choice, 'No Air', which they're all happy with – except for Quinn. The song features Finn and Rachel in the solos, which means they must constantly practise together. Quinn has been coached by Sue to undermine Will by getting Puck and Brittany to leave the team and his group gets smaller by the moment.

Terri frantically hides her fake baby bump while Will comes home. He's got a dose of confidence because he thinks he got one over Sue by failing her Cheerios but the next day, he realises Sue has left him with only three kids and therefore, he can't perform a song. Ever the negotiator, Sue wants her Cheerios back in return for his Glee Club, but Will won't budge – not for the moment.

Terri and her sister Kendra head straight to Dr. Woo, her ob-gyn, to try and blackmail him into going along with their fake-baby plan. Somehow he agrees – clearly there are no ethics in that office.

Quinn corners Rachel and they have a mini-showdown. She wants Rachel to back off from Finn while Rachel knows Quinn has been spying for Sue. Rachel reminds Quinn that, with her pregnancy soon to become public knowledge, she's going to need friends who will stand by her, like the people in New Directions.

The two separate groups are performing for each other. Sue interrupts Will's group barely a note into their number and this is the lead up to the opening scene, where Will and Sue fly at each other in slow motion. Except the Glee Club has had enough and they walk out.

Will is finally at the doctor's office with Terri. Dr.

EPISODE 1.07: 'THROWDOWN'

Woo has gone along with his wife's crazy plan and uses Quinn's ultrasound video to pretend Terri is having a girl, not a boy. Will is thrilled beyond belief.

Sue tells Will that she's stepping down as co-head of Glee and the two have a small reconciliation. She has also found out about Quinn's pregnancy, which she coaxed out of Jacob. Quinn knows this is bad news for her, but the Glee Club rally round during their final song.

Episode 1.07: The Music

Background music: 'O Fortuna', Carmina Burana
   by Carl Orff
Mercedes Jones: 'Hate on Me', Jill Scott
New Directions' Jam Session: 'Ride Wit Me', Nelly
   Rachel Berry and Finn Hudson: 'No Air', Jordin
   Sparks and Chris Brown
Quinn Fabray: 'You Keep Me Hangin' On',
   The Supremes
New Directions: 'Keep Holding On', Avril Lavigne.

GLEEFUL! MOMENT

The Swingle Singers are the vocal group behind the a cappella background music for Glee. Based in London, they produce complex, technically impressive covers of everything from modern songs to classical music.

'MASH-UP'

A student walks around carrying a slushie and each Glee Club member cringes as he goes by. But it turns out that the one person who thought he was immune, popular Jock Finn, is the intended victim. Since joining Glee, Quinn and Finn have tumbled down the social ladder and their status is in major jeopardy.

In the teachers' lounge, Ken and Emma approach Will to ask if he will help them out with their wedding song plans. They want him to create a mash-up of their two completely opposing wedding-song choices and to teach them how to dance.

In the music room, Quinn is helping Finn clean up from the slushie attack and they try and plot ways to regain their status. Will gives the kids their newest song,

'Bust A Move', but when none of the male vocalists steps up to sing the lead, he takes over to show them how it's done.

In her office, Emma is confused as to why Finn and Quinn have come to her for tips on how to be cool – she thought they were the coolest kids in school. She doesn't have much to tell them but when Will walks by, she lets slip a comment about his sunglasses. She covers quickly by telling them that wearing sunglasses is one way to be cool.

Will is about to give Emma her first dance lessons and she arrives in an elaborate Princess Diana-style wedding gown with an extremely long train. She says that she wants to practise dancing in the gown so she's prepared for the wedding. Will starts dancing around her and Emma is entranced but then his feet get tangled up in her train and together, they fall to the ground. They laugh it off, but Ken has spotted them and from his perspective, it doesn't look so innocent. Isn't it bad luck for the groom to see the bride in her dress before the wedding, anyway?

It's football practice but Finn's team remain unimpressed by his juggling of Glee and sports – they obviously don't care that a Glee Club member already helped them win a game. Things get worse as Puck is missing practice for Glee and, with Coach Ken already searching for a way to get back at Will, he orders another practice that conflicts with Glee. In effect, he's making them all choose sports or singing, once and for all.

EPISODE 1.08: 'MASH-UP'

Puck is rehearsing at Rachel's house, accompanying her on the guitar. In a surprise move, they start making out. A flashback shows Puck has been searching for a Jewish girl to date and in a dream he sees Rachel as that girl. For her part, Rachel can't stop thinking about Finn, so she stops things with Puck from going any further. Although it's really because of Finn, she tells him it's because he never steps up at Glee. Puck remedies this right away by singing a solo at the next Glee Club rehearsal. He serenades Rachel in front of everyone – sparking flashes of jealousy from Finn and enabling Quinn to see him in a new light.

The slushie wars continue. Finn and Quinn are trying out the sunglasses' method – except they look ridiculous. And it doesn't help their popularity at all. The entire football team slushies them both, reminding Finn of his upcoming decision between Glee Club and football. Now it seems more like a choice between popularity or loserdom.

At the local news station, suave newscaster Ron asks Sue out on a date. She's flattered and says yes. His attention completely changes her mood – she's borderline nice! She takes dance lessons from Will so that she can accompany Ron to a swing club.

In the locker room, Will tries to apologise to Ken and set the record straight, but Ken is hurting too much over the fact that Emma clearly likes Will to change his mind.

He wants the decision to go ahead as planned. The writing's on the wall when Puck becomes the next victim of a slushie: he can't handle the humiliation so he tells Rachel – in a very nice way – that they can't be together and he's going to choose football over Glee.

Will doesn't really seem to be going along with his promise to Ken of backing down from Emma – in the next scene, he goes wedding-dress shopping with her. She looks stunning in her new gown and as they dance together, they look like the perfect couple. Will reveals to Emma what Ken has done – forced the kids to choose between the team and Glee – and he rushes back to school. The clock ticks toward 3.30 and everyone is anxious, but slowly, they all begin to trickle in – except for Finn.

More slushies, and this time Finn's the attacker. Kurt volunteers to take one for the team. When Finn chickens out, Kurt throws it on himself. He tells Finn it had better be worth it.

Sue suffers a huge blow when she walks in on Rod and the female newscaster kissing on the newsdesk. It's also the first time we've seen her out of her tracksuits – she's in a zoot suit for the swing dance-a-thon. Sue's good mood evaporates in a flash.

Puck and Rachel are also honest with each other on the bleachers (high school stadium seating), admitting who they're really in love with: Puck with Quinn and

Rachel with Finn. But with Quinn carrying Finn's baby, there's no way he will leave her and so neither of them stand a chance.

Will has a heart-to-heart with Finn on the football field. Their chat inspires Finn to talk to his coach and Ken agrees to cancel the conflicting practices.

Naturally, a jilted Sue is not a nice Sue. She dashes Quinn's hopes and dreams by stripping her of her Cheerios' status with immediate effect. Quinn is devastated.

Will admits to Emma that he can't do the mash-up of their wedding songs because they just won't fit together. This is clearly a metaphor for Emma and Ken yet there's still no sign of the wedding being called off.

Even more slushies! But this time Finn has brought them for the Glee Club to enjoy and as an apology for ditching them for football. Will makes the fatal error of admitting he's never been slushied and so New Directions happily oblige.

Episode 1.08: The Music
Will Schuester: 'The Thong Song', Sisqo
Will Schuester: 'Bust A Move', Young M.C.
Rachel Berry: 'What A Girl Wants', Christina Aguilera
Background Music: 'Sing, Sing, Sing', Louis Prima
Puck: 'Sweet Caroline', Neil Diamond
Emma Pillsbury: 'I Could Have Danced All Night',
    My Fair Lady.

'WHEELS'

Times are tight in Lima, Ohio. Quinn has received her first sonogram (ultrasound) bill. Already it's more than she can afford and it's only the first of many. Finn assures her that he's searching for a job but that isn't good enough for Quinn. She needs him to man up and find them some money – she still can't reveal the truth to her parents.

Also, there's not enough money in Glee Club. They need to rent a wheelchair-accessible bus so that Artie can join them as they journey to sectionals. But Principal Figgins refuses to pay up and reveals that Sue has sponsors to pay for the Cheerios' transportation.

So at the Glee Club meeting, Will makes two announcements. The first is that they are going to do a new show tune – 'Defying Gravity'. Kurt is beyond excited as *Wicked* is his favourite musical, but Will automatically gives the solo to Rachel. The second piece of news is that they need to hold a bake sale to raise money for the wheelchair bus. Why don't they have another car wash? It seemed to work the first time around! Including Artie, the team shoot down the idea. But Artie is secretly disappointed: he wants to go on the bus with everyone else.

Kurt announces he wants a shot at the 'Defying Gravity' solo. Will doesn't really believe he should sing a girl's song and so he still gives it to Rachel; he also reiterates that they need to raise money for the wheelchair access as it isn't fair to Artie, so they're going to have a bake sale after all. Not only that, but they're going to experience what it's like to spend time in a wheelchair. He rolls out a chair for each of them to sit in over the next week and to use in a big number.

Their first collective experience of wheelchairs involves getting smacked in the face a lot and not being able to enter the school except by the furthest entrance. It's a real eye-opener. Puck finds Quinn in the home economics' room baking cakes for the fundraiser. He gives her a little bit of money to prove that he's really trying and that he wants to be a father. They start flirting and it ends in a big baking-ingredient food fight. Finn walks in on them and becomes extremely confused.

EPISODE 1.09: 'WHEELS'

Kurt is at his dad's workshop and he vents to him about how Will won't let him sing a girl's song. Well, his father won't stand for that! He's keen to get on his boy's side and so he goes straight to Will and demands Kurt be given a chance to audition. Will agrees and to make sure it's fair to Kurt, he allows the Glee Club to judge as a team. Rachel thinks this will just be a popularity contest but Kurt makes the rest of the team swear they'll be judged on talent.

In Principal Figgins' office with Sue, Will tries to get the head to agree to more wheelchair access to the school. Figgins can't do this, but he makes Sue offer tryouts for Quinn's open position on the Cheerios. ensure the tryouts are fair, he forces Will to moderate.

The bake sale is a horrible failure. No one wants to buy anything from the losers. Only Brittany purchases a cupcake for her friend Becky, who has Down's syndrome. Quinn is still riding Finn hard about not getting a job.

The only bigger failure than the bake sale is the Cheerios' tryouts. No one is impressing Sue: to be fair, none of them are very good. To Will's surprise, Sue chooses the last auditionee – Becky – to join the squad. He suspects an ulterior motive.

Puck gives Finn a good talking-to about not manning up and making money for Quinn. He gives him a million ideas of ways that he can make money. Finn feels undermined and they break out into a fight. Puck storms off after Will breaks them up.

In the auditorium, they are rehearsing the wheelchair number. There's the first hint of attraction between Tina and Artie and we find out how Artie has ended up in a wheelchair: at the age of 8, he became involved in a car accident. He assures Tina that he still has full use of his penis, though!

Kurt is practising hard for the big sing-off with Rachel and manages to hit the elusive high F. In the meantime, his dad receives a threatening phone call and all his insecurities about having a gay son tumble out.

Rachel's wheelchair is broken and Finn is helping her fix it, but Quinn storms up and repeats for the umpteenth time that somehow Finn needs to get her some money. The bake sale is picking up, however, and the cakes are selling like crazy. We find out that Puck has spiked them with marijuana bought from Sandy and the kids can't get enough.

Time for the 'Defying Gravity' battle and it's a close call until Kurt misses the high note that he managed before in practice. Rachel gets the solo.

Proving he's the big daddy, Puck hands Quinn a lot of money for the baby – he really wants her to let him be the father of his child. He admits he stole the money from the cupcake fund but still, he thinks it's proven that he can provide for her. However, Finn interrupts them with a cheque of his own. He's managed to get a job – thanks to Rachel, who convinced him to attend the interview in a wheelchair and get himself hired under Equal Rights.

Puck gives all the money to the wheelchair bus and it amounts to even more than they need. Artie suggests that instead of a bus they buy some wheelchair ramps for the auditorium. Principal Figgins has a surprise for Will, though: Sue has already bought ramps for the school.

Finally, we learn more about Sue. She goes to visit her sister Jean, who has Down's syndrome, just like aspiring cheerleader Becky. In Sue's first truly touching moment, they read together.

Artie and Tina are together after school and they resolve the tension between them by finally kissing. She then admits to faking her stutter, which she only put on because she wanted people to leave her alone. Artie has thought their connection was based on a shared experience of disability and so he rolls away, disgusted.

Kurt reveals to his dad that he lost the tryout with Rachel on purpose because he didn't want to put him through any more aggravation. But Kurt is now comfortable in his skin and willing to put his dad's feelings first.

Finally, we see the results of the wheelchair number – New Directions roll around on the new wheelchair ramps, singing their hearts out to 'Proud Mary'.

Episode 1.09: The Music

Artie Abrams: 'Dancing with Myself', Billy Idol

Rachel Berry and Kurt Hummel: 'Defying Gravity', *Wicked*

New Directions: 'Proud Mary', Creedence Clearwater Revival.

GLEEFUL! MOMENT

Zach Woodlee described the 'Proud Mary' number as the 'scariest' so far that he's choreographed in the show. The cast had to learn how to distribute their weight properly or else they would fall off the wheelchair ramps.

'It was like roller derby,' he told the New York Post. 'All of the actors would fall backwards and hit their heads – particularly Lea Michele, who plays Rachel. You lose your balance really quick when you try to go up a ramp in a wheelchair. Amber Riley, who plays Mercedes, caught an edge going down a ramp and fell off completely. There were pile-ups; there were crashes. Basically, everything that could go wrong, did.'

EPISODE 1.10
'BALLAD'

With a name like 'Ballad', there promises to be more music in this episode. And as Will Schuester announces his first assignment, we're not to be disappointed. He splits the group into pairs by having them draw names out of a hat. The resulting couples must sing a ballad to each other. The pairings are: Puck and Mercedes, Artie and Quinn, Finn and Kurt, Tina and 'Other Asian' Mike Chung and finally, Santana and Brittany, which leaves Rachel to sing with Will. Matt Rutherford, the missing member of New Directions, is unwell.

As Rachel and Will sing 'Endless Love' to each other, Rachel sees her teacher through new eyes and he starts to get nervous as it's clear that she's developing a crush on him.

Quinn is getting dressed up in front of the mirror with her mum. The gown has been specially chosen for her to wear to the Chastity Ball. Her parents are extremely conservative Christians and they want to meet the boy that she's been seeing so that they can give their approval.

After Rachel gives him a present, Will vents his issues with Emma, as he loves to do. This time, he discusses Rachel's schoolgirl crush on him. It's not the first time a student has fallen for him. There was once a girl called Suzy Pepper who fittingly bit down on an extremely hot pepper when Will rejected her and ended up in a medically induced coma. He can't risk the same kind of disaster happening with Rachel and needs to find a way to let her down gently. Emma suggests that he sings his feelings to her.

GLEEFUL! MOMENT

When Kurt is talking with Finn before he sits down to play 'I'll Stand By You' on the piano, he's wearing light-coloured trousers. Later, when there's a close-up of Kurt's hands, he's wearing jeans.

Finn is also reluctant about singing a duet with Kurt. He can't sing to a guy and so he lashes out at Kurt. In reality, he can't stop thinking about his unborn daughter so Kurt says he should sing to his daughter instead. But as he's singing 'I'll Stand By You' to the video of the ultrasound, his mum walks in on him and he confesses to her that Quinn is pregnant.

Will sits Rachel down in the music room but already he's made the mistake of singling her out and making her feel special. His mash-up of songs, obvious as it is, seems to completely pass her by. In fact, he manages to seduce both women in the room, as Emma is there too.

Kurt gives Finn more advice as he's helping him pick out clothes for the first dinner with Quinn's parents. He convinces Finn to sing the truth to the Fabrays, even though it will be against Quinn's wishes. Kurt hopes that he'll be a shoulder to cry on when things go wrong with Quinn and Finn.

In a moment of solidarity, the Glee Club (minus Finn, Rachel and Quinn) decide they'll sing a song to Finn and Quinn to give them support. Puck is disgusted, so he tells Mercedes that he's the real father. Mercedes tells him to back off: she's chosen Finn to be the baby's dad and that's her decision.

It's the day of the big dinner at the Fabrays. Everything is going well until Finn decides to break into his ballad to Quinn's parents. As he sings the line 'You're gonna have my baby', they get the drift and steam starts to pour out of Quinn's dad's ears. Not literally, but he looks livid.

Finn tries to tell the Fabrays that he and Quinn never had sex but obviously, they're not buying it. Quinn's dad kicks them both out of the house. Finn takes her home and luckily his mum says she can stay as long as she wants.

Strangely, it's Suzy Pepper herself who manages to talk some sense into Rachel. She says that she needs to let go of her schoolgirl crush – it's only a product of her insecurities. When Will tries to broach the topic with Rachel, she's already steps ahead of him and the tension is eased.

Kurt tells Finn that his chosen ballad is 'I Honestly Love You' but he's not going to sing it. Instead, he takes Finn to the choir room, where the Glee Club has prepared their ballad to Finn and Quinn: 'Lean On Me'.

Episode 1.10: The Music
Finn Hudson: 'I'll Stand By You', The Pretenders
Will Schuester and Rachel Berry: 'Endless Love',
    Diana Ross and Lionel Richie
Rachel Berry: 'Crush', Jennifer Page
Will Schuester: 'Don't Stand So Close to Me',
    The Police
Will Schuester: 'Young Girl', Gary Puckett &
    The Union Gap
Finn Hudson: '(You're) Having My Baby', Paul Anka
    and Odia Coates
New Directions: 'Lean On Me', Bill Withers.

GLEEFUL! MOMENT

In the mash-up of 'Don't Stand So Close to Me' and 'Young Girl', Will changes the lyrics of 'Young Girl' to make the song more appropriate. The original version says: 'Young girl, get out of my mind/My love for you is way out of line' whereas the Glee lyrics say: 'Young girl, you're outta your mind/ your love for me is way outta line'.

EPISODE 1.11
'HAIROGRAPHY'

Sue Sylvester is back, with a vengeance. In the teachers' lounge, she shows off the cover of *Splits* magazine, which names her the cheerleading coach of the decade. Also, she hasn't forgotten that she's still a Glee Club coordinator and she demands to see a copy of Will's set list. In turn, he has no idea why she's so enthusiastic since she's not really involved in New Directions anymore. But when Brittany starts recording their practices on her video camera, Will realises that Sue plans to sell their routines to the competition. At Emma's insistence, he decides to head straight for the rival schools to plead with them not to cheat.

Jane Addams Academy is where he heads first. No trophy cases and clean-swept floors here, instead he has to pass through lots of security checks to gain access to the school. Their Glee Club coach is Ms Hitchens. She's is in the middle of dealing with one of her delinquent pupils, who has attempted to rob a bank. Will interrupts and as the girl is leaving, she pickpockets his wallet. Ms Hitchens spots this and makes her return it.

Will tries to broach the topic carefully but there's no easy way to accuse another team of cheating. Ms Hitchens is extremely offended that he even dares to insinuate that she would do such a thing. She berates Will for being so insensitive, especially as McKinley High already has such a strong advantage just by virtue of having an auditorium to practise in and money for costumes. Will feels thoroughly chastened and so offers them the opportunity to practise in their music room.

The girls from the reform school come and perform 'Bootylicious' with an extremely showy dance routine. Wide-eyed, Will watches them. Suddenly, he's afraid that New Directions' simpler routines won't cut it in front of the judges. Rachel tries to reassure him and the rest of the team that the Jane Addams' girls are just using 'hairography' – which means they fling their hair around a lot to distract from poor singing or dancing skills.

However, Will clearly hasn't gotten over his fears: his newest song for the group is from the musical *Hair*, complete with shiny long wigs for everyone to wear. Rachel reminds him they're good enough already and they don't need this.

EPISODE 1.11: 'HAIROGRAPHY'

Quinn debates whether she made the wrong decision in cutting Puck out of her baby's life and choosing Finn instead. She needs some time alone with Puck to see if he could actually make a good dad but in order to have that alone time, she must sidetrack Finn – and she realises her best chance is to orchestrate Rachel to distract Finn for her. Quinn convinces Kurt to give Rachel a makeover, a challenge he accepts. Even though he doesn't like Rachel very much, he can't resist the challenge of a makeover.

GLEEFUL! MOMENT

Did you know that the word 'distract' (or variations like 'distracted' and 'distraction') is used 20 times in this episode? Clearly the writers had a central theme!

At home, Will is trying to be intimate with Terri, who of course, isn't having any of it. She realises that she's not going to be able to keep up the charade for much longer unless she can find something else for Will to think about.

In Rachel's bedroom, Kurt is waxing her eyebrows. She's confused as to why Kurt is helping her – she knows he's not her biggest fan, but he says that he's doing it to help the Glee Club as a whole. The conversation moves on to boys and Rachel confesses that the only boy she

261

wants to impress is Finn. Kurt – who loves him too – tells Rachel that she has to amp up the hoochie if she wants to get the guy. Rachel's confused – doesn't Finn prefer good girls like Quinn? But Kurt swears he knows otherwise.

Meanwhile, Terri has figured out the best way to distract Will: she buys him a replica of the old car he used to have in high school. She hopes that working on it will take his mind off pregnancy issues while she sorts out another plan. Everything threatens to blow up in her face, however, when Quinn tells Terri she might want to keep the baby after all. But Terri's sister Kendra comes up with a seemingly brilliant plan – have Quinn babysit Kendra's kids and she'll never want to see a baby again!

Back at school, the Glee Club coach from Haverbrook School for the Deaf comes in to complain to Will about how they weren't invited to the scrimmage with Jane Addams Academy. Because he's deaf in one ear (small pox, don't you know?), it takes Will a while to get the coach to understand that he wants to invite the deaf school in as well.

Rachel's makeover seems to have worked. Finn can't take his eyes off her and Quinn seems a distant memory. He agrees to hang out with her on Friday night to practise their *Hair* routine.

Speaking of that *Hair* routine, Brittany is demonstrating to New Directions how to perform hairography – basically throwing your hair round and round in circles. Will spots Sue looking in on them and he storms over to confront her – except instead, she gives him a good talking-to – she can't believe Will is allowing his kids' talent to be overshadowed by hair-tossing. Wise words!

It's Friday night and Rachel and Finn are together at Rachel's house. Rachel is busy applying as much make-up as her face can take. She comes out of the bathroom all dolled up like Sandy from *Grease*, but Finn's not impressed. In fact, he tells her he preferred it when she looked like a nice girl – he was just telling Kurt that was the look he was attracted to. He leaves and Rachel realises that Kurt has duped her.

Quinn has invited Puck over to babysit and so far they've only succeeded in getting tied up while the kids run round screaming. Puck is always texting on his phone but they manage to get free. To quieten the kids down, they say they're going to perform a 'live music video'. Puck plays guitar while Quinn sings 'Papa Don't Preach' by Madonna. The kids love it, and they demand an encore. When Kendra and Terri come home, they're shocked to find the kids asleep and to learn that they've even had a bath. Puck thinks it's a sign that they would make good parents and even Quinn seems to warm to the idea. In the meantime, Kendra's husband Phil bursts Will's bubble of excitement around his car by pointing out that there won't be room for a baby seat.

Rachel corners Kurt and asks him why he gave her a tarty makeover when he knew full well that Finn preferred the natural look. He admits his own crush on Finn to her, but warns that neither of them can win this battle as they've already lost out to Quinn.

Santana isn't happy with Quinn for babysitting with Puck, whom she still considers her boyfriend – although that doesn't explain why she never had a go at Rachel. Still, Santana reveals that the whole time Puck was at Kendra's house, they were sending flirtatious texts to each other.

The Haverbrook School for the Deaf choir have come to sing for New Directions, except this time New Directions goes first and performs *Hair* for the first time. They look ridiculous and the other choir can't quite believe their eyes. When it's their turn to perform, they sign along to 'Imagine' while one of the kids sings solo. New Directions are so overwhelmed by the simplicity of the performance that they get up and join in. It's a great display of unity and a really touching moment.

Quinn hunts down Puck and grabs his phone out of his locker. There, she finds confirmation that Santana had been telling the truth – the two had been texting while she and Puck were babysitting. Quinn can't believe she was so stupid as to believe Puck could change. She goes straight to Terri and tells her that she'll give up her baby after all because she wants the kid to have a good father figure. Will proves he's just that by trading in his dream car for a beat-up old mini-van but one that can accommodate their new, growing family.

Finn also proves he wants to be honest with Quinn by confessing that he went to Rachel's house. They forgive each other, kiss and make up as Rachel and Kurt wistfully look on.

Will goes to Sue to give her the final set list and thanks her for making him come to his senses. We then see Sue in her office with the two rival coaches and, just as Will predicted, she's giving them a look at the New Directions set list. She even insists they divide up the numbers so it looks like New Directions cheated on both teams.

The last scene sees New Directions return to their roots in a simple rendition of 'True Colors'.

Episode 1.11: The Music
Jane Addams Academy: 'Bootylicious', Destiny's Child
Background Music: 'Don't Make Me Over', Dionne
   Warwick
New Directions' Mash-Up: 'Hair', *Hair*
New Directions' Mash-Up: 'Crazy In Love', Beyoncé
   Feat. Jay-Z
Rachel Berry: 'You're The One That I Want', *Grease*
Haverbrook School: 'Imagine', John Lennon
Quinn Fabray and Puck: 'Papa Don't Preach',
   Madonna
New Directions: 'True Colors', Cyndi Lauper.

GLEEFUL! MOMENT

Michael Hitchcock, who plays Dalton Rumba – coach for the deaf choir – starred with Jane Lynch in the Christopher Guest movies *Best in Show* and *A Mighty Wind*.

'MATTRESS'

McKinley High is all abuzz... yearbook photo season is upon them. All the teachers are primping in the lounge and Will admits that he's forgotten all about it. He chats with Ken and Emma about their upcoming nuptials and finds out the plan to get married in Hawaii has been scrapped because Emma can't bring her own fruit. Instead, they've booked a last-minute date. Emma suddenly realises this conflicts with Sectionals and so she can't come and watch New Directions compete after all.

Sue strolls in with two scary-looking black eyes from a facelift – done especially for her big Cheerios' spread in the yearbook. She also gives Will the news that New Directions won't have a yearbook photo to spare them the humiliation of being vandalised when the book comes out. Will's not happy at all with that idea and vows to fight for his club's photo.

Meanwhile, New Directions themselves are having second thoughts about a yearbook photo. Every yearbook in the past has a picture of Glee Club with insults and drawings scribbled all over it. Kurt suggests maybe it's better they don't have a photo, but Will overrules them, saying they'll have a photo and be proud of it too!

Except getting that space in the yearbook isn't as easy as he anticipates. Always looking for more ways to squeeze the budget, Principal Figgins tells Will that he'll have to pay if he wants a picture. The price is significantly less for a quarter-page so Figgins suggests that Will just picks one or two Glee Club kids to be in the photo. Rachel storms in and also demands a picture in the yearbook as it will be proof of her amazing extracurricular activity. In fact, we learn that she only joins clubs to get in the *Thunderclap*. She treats it more like a paparazzi magazine than a yearbook.

Quinn laments the fact that she's not going to be in the Cheerios' photo now that she's been kicked off the squad. She wants to be remembered as the Cheerios captain and so is determined to get back in the photo.

Will goes to Terri for advice on which tie to wear and subtly broaches the topic of using some money to buy the yearbook photo. She of course says no, but he goes ahead and writes a cheque to Figgins anyway – admittedly, for only a quarter-page size. He then tells the Glee Club that they have to select two captains to be in the shot. Rachel is the only one who volunteers for the job and she's the only one voted in.

Will is back to moaning to his favourite confidante Emma and wishes the kids were more proud to be in Glee. He then asks her if she thinks Ken scheduled the wedding specifically to conflict with sectionals. But Emma doesn't think so and she's convinced Ken is no longer jealous of Will and he's not vindictive.

Rachel's first order of duty as captain is to find a co-captain to appear with her in *Thunderclap*. She can't be the only one representing Glee Club. In turn, she goes to the other members and they all refuse until she appeals to Finn's leadership qualities. He agrees, but chickens out at the last moment after being teased by his football team. Rachel is forced to take the photo alone. However, being the precocious go-getter that she is, Rachel convinces the photographer to let the Glee Club star in a commercial that he happens to be filming for a mattress store. She returns to the Glee Club triumphant at having found them real TV work and everyone is thrilled. They're going to be celebrities!

They arrive at Mattressland for the shoot, where they are all dressed in pyjamas. Rachel suggests revision for the script, which frankly is a little dull and doesn't take full advantage of the Glee Club's talents. So Rachel gets her way and the club sing 'Jump' while bouncing around on the mattresses. The owner loves it!

Uh-oh. Will's at home and searching through all the bedroom drawers for a pocket square to wear with his school photo outfit. That's when he finds one of Terri's pregnancy pads. He storms downstairs and confronts his wife in the kitchen, demanding to see her belly, but she won't show him. At this, he lifts up her shirt and rips the fake bump away. A terrified Terri babbles through the explanation of why she tricked him and explains her plans to pass off Quinn's baby as their own. This understandably makes Will even more upset and he storms out.

Will decides to stay the night in the school. He's confused to find a stack of twelve mattresses in the music room, but he doesn't question the unexpected gift and pulls one down to sleep on.

After filming her segment for 'Sue's Corner', Sue spots the Glee Club's television commercial. She can't believe that after all she has done to bring them down, they have managed to do a better job of doing it all by themselves. Sue goes straight to Principal Figgins and informs him that Glee Club needs to be disqualified as they have done some 'professional' work – and received payment for said work – and therefore cannot compete in an amateur competition. Will is horrified as he didn't even know about the commercial and says they'll gladly return the mattresses (aka the payment) so that they can still perform. Unfortunately, he has already used one of the mattresses so it cannot be returned.

Meanwhile, Quinn goes to Sue in her uniform to demand to be reinstated in the Cheerios' yearbook picture. Sue refuses and Quinn calls her a hypocrite for berating Glee Club for accepting payment while the cheerleaders get tons of free stuff. Afraid of Quinn going to Principal Figgins to brag about the swag, Sue offers her position back, but Quinn decides she doesn't want to be in the cheerleading picture after all. She prefers to be represented where she feels the most comfortable – Glee Club.

GLEEFUL! MOMENT

In the caption for the Glee Club photo, Puck's first name is written as 'Nathan', although we know it's really 'Noah'.

Emma and Will talk about his imploding marriage, and Emma empathises with his wife a little – not with her methods, but with her motives. She can understand why Terri would do anything to keep Will... and admits that if she were his wife, she would probably do the same.

Will then realises that he is the one who has to resign

from Glee Club: after all, he used the mattress, not the kids. That means they can still go to sectionals although it will have to be without their favourite Glee Club coordinator. It looks like Will's dreams are over as he's excluded from the picture. True to their word, upon publication of the *Thunderclap*, the football team scribble all over the images of the Glee Club. But that's okay – they're in it together.

Episode 1.12: The Music
Rachel Berry: 'Smile', Lily Allen
Rachel Berry: 'When You're Smiling', Louis Armstrong
Background Music: 'You Might Think', The Cars
New Directions: 'Jump', Van Halen
New Directions: 'Smile', Charlie Chaplin.

GLEEFUL! MOMENT

The original working title for this episode was 'Once Upon a Mattress'. In 2005, Matthew Morrison starred in a TV version of the play, *Once Upon a Mattress*.

'SECTIONALS'

N ow that Will's been disqualified from running Glee Club, New Directions is nervous about who will replace him. Rachel bounds in with a new theory, although in reality she's behind the times. She thinks that there's something strange about the way Puck is so protective over Quinn, rushing to her aid at the same time as Finn when she falls down. Of course, the other kids already know about Puck and Quinn but they don't want Rachel to find out or else she'll tell Finn and that would be the end of Glee. We also learn there might be more going on between Santana and Brittany than meets the eye.

Emma is the one who has volunteered to take over Glee Club. She pushed the wedding back to be able to attend the competition. Although she says she's doing it for the kids, really, we all know better.

But New Directions don't realise how quickly Rachel moves. She finds Quinn by her locker and casually asks her if she's had the baby tested for Tay-Sachs, a condition only passed on by Jews. This prompts Quinn to confront Puck in the music room while Rachel looks on, intrigued.

Emma is introduced as the faculty advisor. She can't help with the set list, though so the Glee Club will have to do it for themselves. The first argument comes over the choice of the ballad. Rachel is, of course, happy to volunteer one of her own ballads, but Mercedes wants to try. Mercedes gets up and sings 'And I Am Telling You I'm Not Going' from *Dreamgirls* and the whole room (not to mention those watching at home!) is awed by her performance. Even Rachel agrees it's the perfect song to bring down the house during the competition.

Finally, everything seems to be going well for Glee Club. Finn shares his excitement about the sectionals with Rachel. For some reason, Rachel believes this is the ideal time to tell him about her suspicions surrounding Puck and Quinn and that leads to Finn beating Puck up in rehearsal. Although it comes out that Rachel is the one who told Finn, the revelation hardly matters in the wake of Finn's anger towards Quinn and Puck. Finn dumps Quinn and Glee Club.

EPISODE 1.13: 'SECTIONALS'

Rachel tries to apologise to Quinn. She's strangely serene about the apparent betrayal because really all Rachel did was tell Finn the truth, which is what Quinn should have done all along. Rachel leaves Quinn to herself, but then Puck arrives. Puck is relieved that they can now openly do the parenting thing together, but Quinn surprises him by saying she wants to go it alone.

It's time for sectionals, but hardly the joyous bus ride that Will envisaged. For one, Will isn't even allowed to go on the bus and Finn has been replaced by Jacob to make up the numbers.

Arriving at sectionals, they find out that they're going last. Rachel is happy: first or last is best. That is, until they see the other teams perform. Jane Addams start to sing Mercedes' balladand then they all get in wheelchairs and sing 'Proud Mary'. Obviously, the team has copied New Directions' set list, but the judges won't know that. Emma calls Will and tells him how distraught the team is and how she can't hold it together. He reassures her that he has a plan. On his way to fulfilling said plan, he spots Sue. They have another massive row and Will vows to show her up for the fraud she is.

The plan takes Will to the boys' locker room, where Finn is clearing out his stuff. Will tells him what's going on at the competition and implores him to go to sectionals and be a leader. He leaves his car keys behind on the bench and waits to see if Finn will make the right decision.

Emma confronts the other two Glee coaches, saying they should be ashamed for teaching their kids that cheating is the only path to victory. They pull out some lame excuses, but it's Emma who has the last word.

Things just get worse as the Haverbrook Choir sing 'Don't Stop Believin'', their new song. Rachel rounds on the three Cheerios, claiming they were the ones who leaked the set list. Brittany admits she did give the set list – although she's too dumb for them really to blame her – and Santana makes the surprising admission that Glee Club is really her favourite part of the day.

Luckily, New Directions has a massive repertoire to choose from, as we have seen all season. Sue didn't think of that! Mercedes gives up her ballad for Rachel, who knows the perfect song. Quinn suggests 'Somebody to Love', but it's still not enough. Finally, Finn saves the day when he walks in with sheet music to a new song. Can they really learn a whole new routine in the few minutes before they're about to go on? Apparently they can! This doesn't mean that Finn has forgiven anyone but he isn't prepared to see all their hard work go to waste.

Emma sits in the audience, on the phone to Will. Their ballad begins and Rachel appears in the audience, belting out 'Don't Rain On My Parade'. The audience gives a standing ovation in appreciation of her amazing performance.

After that, New Directions breaks into Finn's song

choice: 'You Can't Always Get What You Want'. Will listens to the performance through the phone and his eyes well up with tears of pride. They've pulled it together, even in the face of the other teams' blatant cheating.

The judging panel consists of three judges who really couldn't care less about the outcome – the complete opposite of the kids who see the competition as deadly serious! As the Glee kids listen at the door, it doesn't sound good.

Ms Hitchens, the Jane Addams' coach, comes over to congratulate them and to say that she's going to come clean to the judges. Except that when the judges come out, they don't want to listen to anyone else's opinion: they've made their decision.

Will is getting dressed for the wedding. Terri comes home early and the two have an awkward post-blowout first meeting. She pleads to have him back and tries to show that she's changing by going to see a therapist. It's too late for Will, though – he just can't see himself loving Terri again.

When Will enters the reception with a gift, it's empty – except for Emma in her gown. When Will asks where everyone is, she explains that Ken has called the wedding off. For him, the last straw was her decision to move the wedding for sectionals. She also comes clean about why she did sectionals – for him, not the kids. Her heart will always belong to Will while she works at

William McKinley High and that's why she's decided to quit. He tells her that he's left Terri, but Emma knows it's all too soon.

Principal Figgins learns of the cheating from the other coaches and he confronts Sue. She tries to deny it, but he strips her of her cheerleading coach title *and* suspends her from the school. Sue cannot believe it, but we know this won't be the end. Will is given back his position as head of Glee now that Figgins has cleared up the mattress incident. Sue hands it to Will and although it may look like he's won the battle, she's going all out for the war.

Will walks into the music room, back in his rightful position as head of Glee Club. The New Directions team are there and they surprise him with the sectionals trophy. He's over the moon for them, but reminds the students that now they have regionals to worry about.

New Directions sit him down for a special performance. As they belt out 'My Life Would Suck Without You', Will knows where he's supposed to be. He rushes round the school in search of Emma, who has packed up her guidance counsellor office and is about to leave. In the closing moments of the show, they finally kiss. What will happen next?

EPISODE 1.13: 'SECTIONALS'

Episode 1.13: The Music

Mercedes Jones: 'And I Am Telling You I'm Not Going', *Dreamgirls*

Rachel Berry: 'Don't Rain on My Parade', *Funny Girl*

New Directions: 'You Can't Always Get What You Want', The Rolling Stones

New Directions: 'My Life Would Suck Without You', Kelly Clarkson.

GLEEFUL! MOMENT

Did you notice that in the final number, 'My Life Would Suck Without You', New Directions work in dance moves from songs they have performed previously?

Repeated dance moves:

Cowboy Hats from 'Last Name'

Mercedes on the chairs from 'Hate On Me'

Jumping around from 'Jump'

Kurt, Tina and Brittany do the 'Single Ladies' dance

Quinn, Santana and Brittany from 'Say A Little Prayer For You'

Boys fist-pumping and rocking their shoulders from 'It's My Life/ Confessions Part II'

Girls do halos from 'Halo/Walking on Sunshine'

A couple walking in between two lines of people from 'Somebody to Love'

Standing in lines facing each other from 'Keep Holding On'

In-out dance and the girls slap their legs from 'Push It'

Thinker position from 'Sit Down, You're Rocking the Boat'

Leg-slapping from 'I Kissed A Girl'

Brittany does hairography from 'Hair/Crazy In Love'

Artie tips his wheelchair from 'Proud Mary'.

OFFICIAL TWITTERS

FOX Official *Glee* Twitter: @GLEEonFox
Lea Michele: @msleamichele
Cory Monteith: @frankenteen
Amber Riley: @MsAmberRiley
Jenna Ushkowitz: @IJennaUsh
Kevin McHale: @druidDUDE
Chris Colfer: @chriscolfer
Mark Salling: @mark_salling
Dianna Agron: @alittlelamb
Harry Shum: @iharryshum

CAN YOU DESCRIBE GLEE?

Do you have difficulty in describing *Glee* to your friends? You're not alone! Here's what some people have had to say about the series:

'I saw elements of the movie *Election*, plus *Fame* and *Friday Night Lights*, with a bit of *The Wonder Years* thrown in, only it's not nostalgia. *Glee* is all the best parts of all the above, plus music and dancing and great characters and really witty material.'
– Allison Waldman, *TV Squad*

'I don't know how to describe it to people. You just have to watch it. You can't compare this show to anything; it's so fresh and original.'
– Matthew Morrison at Comic-Con 2009

'[It's] a cross between *The Breakfast Club* and *Grease*.'
– CNN.com

'The show follows a bunch of oddballs in an American high-school choir. And mixing catty comedy and camp West End versions of Beyoncé's "Single Ladies" and Journey's "Don't Stop Believin'", it makes *X-Factor* look like *Newsnight Review*.'
– Kate Faithful, *News of the World*

'I describe *Glee* as a cross between *Freaks and Geeks* and *High School Musical*.'
– Emmerson Parker, *If Magazine*

'The new musical-comedy drama *Glee* dresses like *High School Musical* and has the heart of *Porky's*.'
– David Hinckley, *NY Daily News*

'*Glee* is like all the best bits of *Election*, *The Faculty*, *Heathers* and *Mean Girls*.'
– Anna Pickard, *Guardian*

'It's High School Cynical.'
– The Chris Moyles Show, Radio One

CAN YOU DESCRIBE GLEE?

'It's a musical comedy-drama full of misfits, homosexuals and bitches. It's... lovely. It's like *High School Musical*, but written by evil people.'
– Caitlin Moran, *The Times*

'At its best *Glee* is an impeccable collision of the romcom, the teen soap, the satire, and the late-night drama. In short, I'm hooked.'
– The *Independent*

'It's wickedly funny and it's about heroes and underdogs. We need [audiences] to know this isn't *High School Musical*. It's also for people who watched *The* OC or who liked the movie *Election*.'
– Joe Early, executive VP in charge of marketing for FOX

'*Glee* is like the bubonic plague. We are everywhere.'
– Jane Lynch, at the 16th Annual SAG Awards

'[*Glee*] is like *High School Musical*... if *High School Musical* was punched in the stomach and had its lunch money stolen.'
– Cory Monteith